The Third Way

A Vision of a Fair Economic System
Beyond Neoliberalism and Socialism

Rainer Grunert

The True Meaning of Life

We are visitors on this planet.
We are here for ninety or one hundred years at the very most.
During that period, we must try to do something good,
something useful, with our lives.
If you contribute to other people's happiness,
you will find the true goal, the true meaning of life.[1]

Tenzin Gyatso, 14th Dalai Lama (born 1935)

Contents

1 The Vision of a Fair Economic System

True peace also means economic development and social justice, means protection of the environment and damming of worldwide drug trafficking, means democracy, variety, and dignity, respect of human rights and rule of law and much, much, more.[2]

Kofi Atta Annan
(Seventh Secretary-General of the United Nations, Nobel Peace Prize recipient, born 1938)

From Idea to Vision

Start by doing what's necessary,
then what's possible,
and suddenly you will achieve the impossible.

Saint Francis of Assisi
(founder of the Order of Friars Minor, 1181-1226)

In November 2008, at the beginning of the worldwide financial crisis, as the first signs of the collapse of the American real estate market began to be recognizable, I met with a friend and we talked about possibly writing a book for a general audience about the economic interrelationships of the crisis. We philosophized about human nature and its inclination toward greed. We also talked about people's distinct sense of fairness, about money and its function as a medium of exchange, about the fact that it is meant to constantly be moving, to constantly be in flux.

At the time, I was not planning to develop a vision of a fair economic system, let alone write a book about it.

I am a psychologist, management expert, and non-fiction author and I have a coaching practice. Before this book, I have written about relationships and have published a philosophical parody of the power of wishing.[3] I am neither an economist, nor a capital or interest theoretician, nor have I been involved with such topics to a great extent until now. As the saying goes: life is full of surprises.

I packed up some relevant literature and printed out hundreds of pages from the internet to read through at my favorite spot on the beach in Goa, India. I wanted to develop the first draft of an easily accessible book about the economic crisis.

I know India well; I travel around the country often and have spent considerable time in several cities there. Poverty and beggars are as much a part of everyday life here as incredible affluence, and at this point they only reach the periphery of my awareness. Anyone who has spent time and traveled in India knows that begging is often organized by petty crime groups. It was not in fact the beggars' poverty that was so thought-provoking to me – it was the lack of opportunity for those people who actually do have work but never make it over the poverty line: migrant workers.

One situation caught my eye: a man and woman whose ages I could not define standing on the edge of a path, tearing up the earth with a pick-ax. They were using a bowl instead of a shovel to push the soil off to one side. Their few belongings – consisting of a worn, checkered blanket, a small gas stove, and a pot – lay on the side of the street. They always kept these objects with them as they moved from one area to the next. Even though they worked all day long, they would never have more than very modest lives. They would remain the underdogs.

India is a country of extremes. It is quite possible that a high-speed internet cable was going to be placed in the ditch that the two migrant workers had to dig. The country has a middle class of about 320 million people who strive toward western standards. Along with Russians, the people in India's upper class are among the wealthiest in the world.

The hopelessness of the people's situation is what affected me the most in this experience – the fact that, despite all their work and effort, they could not escape their poverty. For me, it is an analogy for the whole world, for the worldwide economic system. It has to do with the fact that it is possible to make money from money and get rich. Meanwhile other people, despite diligent work, often remain poor. It has to do with the ownership of land and the arbitrary distribution of its raw materials, which we cannot undo even with the most well-intentioned reforms.

It seems that something doesn't make sense in the system as a whole.

If so, however, then small adjustments will not help. Neither will new changes to a few parameters, nor pumping in the taxpayers' capital. Multi-billion dollar economic stimulus packages will not have a lasting effect because the next, even bigger crisis will already be on its way. And, in my opinion, the traditional methods for recovery of the system will ultimately fail – if not this time then during the next crash or the one after that. Therefore, it does not make sense for me to try, dear reader, to explain the current economic model to you. Instead, I have delved into the literature on the topic and have hit upon many exciting ideas and possibilities for change which I will outline in this book.

All of my proposals will follow the principle that one cannot take anything away from any other person in order to distribute it to another – and yet in the end there will be only winners.

In the next chapter, "The Human Being – There is Enough for Everyone," I will discuss certain aspects of human nature and show why every proposal for change that does not incorporate these aspects will fail.

In Chapter 3, "Land – The Fair Distribution of Real Estate and a Worldwide Unconditional Income," I will describe how we can increase the worldwide standard of living, first and foremost for the poor, without taking anything from anyone, whether they be rich or poor.

And in the chapter "Money and Why it Only Works If We Believe in It," I will introduce a monetary system that does freeze not up even under adverse conditions and at the same time has no inclination toward the usual crises like inflation or deflation.

The models presented were developed long before I was even born. They go back to the French economist and Marx critic Pierre-Joseph Proudhon, the Belgian-Argentinean businessman Johann Silvio Gesell, and the British economist John Maynard Keynes. I have boiled them down for you and, where I saw appropriate, dusted them off. Wherever it was possible, I made connections to modern financial instruments and a global world.

Something is Amiss

It is the nature of every person to err,
but only the fool perseveres in error.

Marcus Tulliius Cicero
(Roman orator and writer, 106-43 BCE)

I am like many other people: I barely understand my tax returns and the official forms from the internal revenue service. I even have difficulties calculating my retirement fund and completing the necessary customs declaration when I ship a large Christmas package from where I live in Switzerland to Germany.

But is it actually a failure on my part, or is this incapacity possibly caused by the fact that for every rule there are five exceptions, eight exclusions, and on top of it all significant room for interpretation? Or are some things so complicated just because they have gotten out of hand – because generations of politicians and bureaucrats have tried to abide by the existing system and, in the end, have lost sight of its essence?

The former German Chancellor Helmut Schmidt is said to have once described the complexity of such details saying: *"It may be easier to govern a country than to read an electricity bill."*[4] He was right, and therefore I will not let this vision of mine get lost in details. Although this might raise a host of questions and leave readers unsatisfied, my work here is concerned with the vision and not with the details of its implementation.

Visions and ideas are, by their very nature, unformed things. They are the fruit in the wine press and differ considerably from a packaged, matured, and labeled bottle of wine. They pose more questions than they answer, and that is how it should be: A vision should evoke consideration beyond familiar trains of thought. Do not judge this vision of a fair economic system on its immediate feasibility, but consider it as one of many potential new models.

When you imagine the worldwide economy with all the effects of globalization and its intricate flow of capital, it is helpful to compare it to complex clockwork.

The purpose of a clock is to display the time, the more precisely the better. A clock that does not work reliably – one that runs faster or slower every now and then or stops altogether – is one that fails to do its job. It is not dependable and is either broken or has a fundamental flaw in design. You can bring this clock to a clockmaker and have it repaired. Maybe he will open it up, oil it, and replace a few gears. If the clock still runs incorrectly and has the same problems, then you can assume that the clockmaker does not know his trade well.

Maybe at that point you send the clock to the manufacturer. The engineers set to work to correct the faulty mechanism. You get the clock back, and it works for a while – even though now it has become a little larger because many new gears have been added. The specialists in the clock factory have not addressed the basic problem in the clockwork. Instead, they built a makeshift repair that works for now but that makes everything more complicated and inscrutable.

The global economic and monetary system functions just like the clock in this example: It has never really worked because since there have been economies, there have been crises, and they happen with increasing frequency as the world grows closer together.

As the world becomes more interconnected, its network of interdependence becomes more inscrutable, and its interrelations become more incomprehensible. At this point, there are too many gears in the mechanism and specialists themselves no longer know the function of particular parts and their influences on the whole. The turning of one unassuming little wheel can, through the course of intricate paths of cause and effect, result in catastrophe.

How else could a single bank like Lehman Brothers cause a worldwide collapse of the financial system? A catastrophe which almost no one predicted because very few people even understood what other parts of the mechanism the Lehman Brothers gear would affect. The complexity of the world economic system now by far exceeds the understanding of its creators and engineers. It is a colossal machine which grows and becomes exponentially more complex with every crisis.

In a crisis, the system is not changed. Instead, more gears are added. New regulations are introduced and new agreements reached in the hope that the next crisis will not be so bad. Referring to this situation, the British economist John Maynard Keynes said: "*In the long run, we are all dead. Economists set themselves too easy, too useless a task if in tempestuous seasons they can only tell us that when the storm is past the ocean is flat again.*"[5]

What else should they say? They are not to blame, nor are the investment bankers on Wall Street, the jobholders who set aside their money in retirement funds, nor the Indian migrant workers.

There are no culprits because the flaw lies in the system.[i] A clock that does not function properly because it was poorly designed cannot and will not run correctly despite all adjustments – that is just the way it is.

The only way out is to design a new clock, a clock whose task it is to show the time in a simple, practical, and easily understood way with the fewest gears possible. A clock that all people on earth understand and that functions reliably. Applied to economy, this means: an economic system which is as comprehensible to Africans as it is for Americans, an economic system that both the rich and poor feel is fair, and that gives everyone the opportunity for development, growth, and wealth.

---

[i] Some readers may have difficulty with this statement and may wish that I would divide the world into groups of "good" small investors and a handful of "bad" bankers. It's not as simple as that: The fact is that – without the small investors' money, without normal consumers' demands for life insurance, for retirement funds, for his pocket book, and any other provisions for old age – there would not be speculation to the extent in which it exists today.

A Fair Economic System is Simple, Practical, and Universally Understandable

It annoys men to find that the truth is so simple,
they should consider that they still have enough energy
to use it to their advantage.[6]

Johann Wolfgang von Goethe
(German Poet, 1749–1832)

How can we create a simple, practical economic system that everyone can understand when everything is so complex and the situation looks so forbidding and deadlocked?

The first step is to recognize that we can make temporary repairs but that they will not erase the problems. This step alone may be difficult for economists and bankers – it requires the concession that finding a landing strip while flying blind is more related to luck than to wisdom

The second step is to allow our perspectives to broaden. We should not just look at one single little gear within the system; we should develop a feel for the mistakes and the possibilities in its construction. In psychology, this is known as a meta-perspective – taking a step back in order to see one's own problems while still keeping the big picture in mind.

The third step is more difficult because it necessitates that we transcend our assumptions and customs and think outside the box. It requires that we set aside for a moment everything that we take for granted – everything that we accept as economic laws of nature – and clear our perspectives for new thoughts and visions. We also have to put our internal censor, who asks immediately about feasibility, momentarily on hold.

The fourth and most difficult step is to put on a "veil of ignorance." This term was coined by John Rawls (1921-2002), an American philosopher, who developed one of the most important theories of fairness and justice.[7] To put on the "veil of ignorance" means that, with decisions involving fairness, we have to free ourselves from our societal and financial status, our mental and physical abilities, particular biases, notions of good and evil, skin color, race, gender, and religion.

Fifth and lastly we have to practice patience, because if we create a new economic system, it will take generations for its effects to lead to lasting change and to become the reality that Kofi Annan envisioned.

In his book, *The Wealth of Nations*,[8] the Scottish moral philosopher and founder of classical political economics Adam Smith (1723-1790) poses the question: What is more meaningful, collective, societal happiness or personal, individual happiness? After much consideration, Smith arrived at the following answer: collective, societal happiness is maximized when every individual tries, from the framework of his or her own ethical system, to increase his or her personal happiness.

This is the key to my vision of a fair economic system: the connection between individual pursuit of personal happiness and its effects on collective, worldwide happiness.

When we recognize that the economy's clockwork has a few basic flaws in design and we put ourselves behind the "veil of ignorance", suddenly the doors to unforeseen thoughts and visions can open. We can then begin, without major intervention in forms of government or politics, to construct a fair economic system based purely on economics and the laws of the market.

The work of building this economic system involves, to a large extent, what Adam Smith called the "invisible hand". It includes market forces and regulators that are influenced by human nature – not because someone decided to do something good or fair, but because in the actions people take for themselves as well as for a group, they follow genetic programs to a great extent.

I will refrain from using numbers and calculations in this book. First of all, these numbers are not readily available, and second, almost none of us can imagine the magnitudes in which economic actions transpire. Most people cannot conceive of billions and trillions, neither in their intellectual universes nor in their wallets: these are dimensions which exceed the powers of comprehension.

Economists, statisticians, and mathematicians, however, who work with large numbers fearlessly and undauntedly, will find a large part of the information that is necessary for future calculations on the websites of the CIA Factbook,[9] the Worldbank, [10] the International Monetary Fund, [11] and the United Nations.[12]

2 The Human Being –
There is Enough for Everyone

The frog that lives in a well
judges the heavens
according to the width of the well's edge.[13]

Mongolian proverb

A change of lasting stability in the existing system will only have a chance if we consider human beings' characteristics and their motivations. Only when we place the human being in the center – with all his acquisitiveness, his propensity to hoard, but also his feeling for justice, his fear, and his compassion – will we find a good and reasonable solution for everyone.

This chapter is about the human being, his behavior as an individual, a group member, as well as a world citizen. No economic system can ignore him: as difficult as it may be, the system has to reconcile greed, compassion, fairness, and fear.

Wealth or Poverty

Because all striving springs from want or deficiency,
from dissatisfaction with one's own state or condition –
it is therefore suffering so long as it is not satisfied.
No satisfaction, however, is lasting; on the contrary,
it is always merely the starting point of fresh striving.[14]

Arthur Schopenhauer
(German philosopher, 1788–1860)

Virtually everyone knows the allegory about the perspective of the pessimist and the optimist: for a pessimist sees the glass as half empty and the optimist as half full. This may be the case with beer glasses, but when we observe the world from the outside – with all its beauty, its resources, its hardship and suffering – this perspective makes no sense.

Let us look from outer space, for example from the International Space Station (ISS): on the earth we see a blue planet partly covered in clouds orbiting through the darkness of space. The question of whether the earth is half full or half empty – whether there are enough or too few resources for all its people – does not apply: There is no alternative to life and cooperation on this planet. That fact will not change with the generations to come.

Even if skeptics complain that we have, in our depletion of nature and plundering of natural resources, already used over half of what was once available to us, it still makes little sense to take a pessimistic perspective. There is, after all, nothing with which to fill up the half empty glass at hand – there is no bottle from which we can pour. We will obtain nothing more than what we already have: this very planet with precisely the number of resources that are currently available.

Let us leave our imagined perspective and land with both feet on the ground. We are immediately overcome with fear: So many people and everyone wants a piece of the pie. Will it be enough for everyone? And most importantly: Is there enough for me? Distributive justice therefore, quickly becomes a demand on others, on those who have more than I do. It becomes a demand on people with a lot of wealth or property, regardless of the fact that, from the perspective of the migrant workers, every citizen in the developed countries counts as a wealthy person.[i] Therefore, we should raise the question: Do our ideas and concepts of fairness and justice arise from a sense of scarcity or a sense of abundance? If they come from a sense of scarcity, they will be influenced by envy and jealousy and will carry elements of revenge.

Affluent children's anger against the established order, which is seen from time to time in the shattered glass of windows and burnt cars in western cities, is nothing more than childish fear of missing out disguised in the costumes of urban rebels. But protection of vested rights also comes from a feeling of scarcity, whether or not it deals with the fear known as the "yellow peril" in earlier times, the strengthening of the right of asylum, or the Employment Protection Act in Europe.

With a feeling of scarcity, an emptiness in the heart, all considerations in regard to distributive justice will fail. They inevitably fall short since they require that, in order for someone to obtain something, it has to be taken from someone else.

This is the root of the problems of traditional concepts like socialism, communism, Maoism and other "equity-isms", but also the difficulties of Christian social ethics, even those in social democracy. Everyone wants to take something from someone else in order to distribute it to other people.

However, there is not just one single pie – our western, developed world. There is rather an amount of unused ingredients, from which bread, pie, and cookies can be made.

That however, demands a shift in perspective. The frog in the well from the quote that introduces this chapter has to broaden his focus from "distributing" to "gaining." He can only accomplish this, however, by leaving the well and recognizing that the sky is bigger than he ever dared to imagine it might be. This knowledge requires effort on the frog's part. He has to get up and leave the brackish floor of the well. He has to take a

---

[i] Unfortunately, even in the developed countries poverty is increasing and the gap between rich and poor grows wider every day. It should be clear that the threat of unemployment or of receiving welfare is in no way comparable to the poverty in the third world. In developed countries, money is transferred from above to below – in the third world there is death.

chance and climb to the light on the slippery wall. Perhaps he will slide back down. Perhaps he will have to make many attempts. If he does not give up, he will climb all the way to the edge of the well. There he will be rewarded not only with new awareness about the size of the sky, but also with his own freedom.

The German philosopher Peter Sloterdijk said, "People dream of free income; they want to be rich, but without giving anything."[15] But nothing is free. Even though death does not cost anything, we pay for it with life itself. We have to make an effort, even if we only change our perspectives.

When we have changed our perspectives and recognize that there are enough resources for everyone, then the question of taking from other people simply does not arise. Instead, we have to consider how to tap this immense wealth and distribute it fairly.

And another thing: All approaches to distribution from top to bottom, all confiscation of property and socialization have created more misery than they eliminated. The noble ideals of revolutionary justice often conceal nothing more than revenge of the alleged underdog.

A long-term solution, therefore, has to serve everyone's interests. It has to be formed from a collective vision: Prosperity for everyone is possible, and it can happen without even one person losing one thing – without anything being taken from anyone.

There is enough for everyone. We just don't see it yet.

The Many Sides of People –
The Homo Economicus Problem

Is not the ideal an avoidance,
an escape from the what has been,
or from what is?[16]

Jiddu Krishnamurti
(Indian spiritual teacher, 1895–1986)

If everything is so simple, why don't we see it?

Doesn't the human being that scientists define as *Homo economicus*, the human being who thinks economically, automatically have to recognize his own interests and behave accordingly?

A person who thinks purely economically – a rational machine that takes all possible factors into account and draws from them the maximized profit – would only be possible on paper and in mathematical models. That is also the reason why most economic models make false predictions. People are more complex than that. They operate on considerably more than profit maximization and reason. And that is a good thing, because otherwise we would live in an even more unjust world, a world of pure egoism without compassion.

People are better than is commonly believed – this applies to every person, whether investment banker or anti-globalization activist, whether rich or poor. For the most part, they act not out of reason or insight, but out of genetic programs that were optimized over millennia and stood the test of time in their propagation over the whole planet. These systems are neither good nor bad; instead they have an evolutionary function and often contain contradictions and conflicts. Furthermore, these systems are not set in stone. They are exceedingly flexible programs that act on and can develop at both individual and societal levels.

Charles Darwin, the founder of evolutionary theory, recognized the interaction of the different levels of evolution and wrote: "Within a clan, honest people do not have distinct advantage over dishonest ones. However, clans of honest people will easily triumph over other groups. This is natural selection."[17]

There are therefore two levels on which natural selection and human development act. One is the individual level, on which it doesn't matter whether I lie or tell the truth, whether I am greedy or a good Samaritan. The Mafia live in villas on the beach while good people live in cheap cars on the street. The other level, however, is the group level: If there were only Mafia groups, then humanity would have died out a long time ago because, either over a short time or a long one, we would have destroyed each other completely.

It seems that the average person has more heart than that.

In a certain way, the heart beats for itself: it is self-serving, egoistic, and will capitalize on every opportunity for itself. In biology, this is called self-preservation. It is the source of greed and the feeling that one can never have enough.

In a certain way, there is never enough, particularly if it involves storing up meat and nuts for the winter and competing with every other individual. Here, being strong is what counts because the situation is a matter of sheer survival. And even if your barn is already full, it is never a bad idea to continue to store in other places. You never know how severe the winter will be and how long it will last. Egoism and the tendency to hoard seem to be human qualities, seem to be necessary for survival. Therefore, we should be wary of pointing the finger at someone who is just following biological programs.[i]

The other heart that beats in us is not cold and individualist, but its beat rather has an innate feeling for fairness. One single person is too weak to overcome every challenge in the world alone and to guarantee that his genes will be passed on to the next generation. There are challenges that

---

[i]: Here, a few readers will raise the objection that each person has the freedom of choice, that he can behave greedily or can moderate himself. This assumption presupposes free will – that one has a will and sense of discipline that are stronger than any genetic predisposition. In religious and spiritual terms, this ability is known as "consciousness"; new neurophysiology research, for example by Wolf Singer, the director of the Neurophysiology Department at the Max-Planck Institute for Brain Research in Frankfurt am Main, denies that this freedom of choice exists. See also: "Verschaltungen legen uns fest. Wir sollten aufhören, von Freiheit zu sprechen." In: Geyer, Christian (Ed..): *Hirnforschung und Willensfreiheit. Zur Deutung der neuesten Experimente.* Suhrkamp, Frankfurt 2004, p. 30-65.

can only be solved collectively.

This idea is very old. Lions and wolves, for example, hunt for prey in groups. Why would animals hunt in packs if they came away with empty stomachs?[18] New research confirms the existence of genetic faculties that promote both individual well-being and fairness in virtually all animals that live in groups.[19]

These two genetic faculties are often in conflict when our consciences come into play, and they are affected by a third component: the solidarity with people who are physically closer to us and with whom we assume ourselves to be culturally similar. This component explains why the donations for the tsunami catastrophe in Thailand were so much more than expected – there were a few fellow citizens affected – and why we are not interested in much larger natural catastrophes, the earthquake in China, for example, which result in even more casualties. This is not disgraceful. It is just following the program that causes many of us to feel closer to our own group than to a foreign one.

People are therefore neither good nor bad. Instead, they follow different, sometimes conflicting programs. They have heated discussions about justice and fairness. They point their fingers at others and then toss and turn at night with a guilty conscious. The next day, despite their better judgment, despite their knowledge of wage dumping and cheap imports from the third world, they buy cheap merchandise from discount stores.

We recognize that we cannot change this, but that we have to integrate the all-too human in a new economic system. We have to consider the privilege of individualism and the tendency toward egoism, as well as all people's extremely keen sense of fairness.

We should therefore be exceedingly careful in criticizing people for their greed. Its cause is, after all, biological programming. Instead, we should make an effort to take everyone with us into the boat. Even if we are afraid that we won't all fit, even if capsizing and drowning seem possible.

The fact is: If we do not find a solution supported by everyone, we will sink, one way or another.

Fairness but not Uniformity

Humanity achieves more when, instead of commending uniformity, we pay respect to the miracle that is diversity.[20]

Hans Kasper
(German writer, born 1916)

The notion of fairness connotes "honesty" and "a sense of order" and is equated with generally accepted justice and reasonableness.[21] Fairness, therefore, does not mean uniformity and is not a call for social leveling that would put us all into a single category. We are, after all, not all the same – not as people and not as nations. However, there has to be a form of equal rights that unites us all as people.

What doesn't work, as has already been described, is social leveling that involves taking something away from people in order to distribute it to others. Such an action would inevitably provoke huge protest. Why should some people have to give something up, without receiving something in return? On the other hand, strong discrepancies like excessive wealth next to bitter poverty engender unease and outrage, and rightly so. They are not fair and jar our natural sense of justice.

Obviously, this is a dilemma. The problem is not our consciences or senses of justice because we cannot free ourselves of those things. We can only decide with whom we want to compare ourselves and what we want to see.

Investment advisors and bankers, whose sense of fairness we like to discuss in great detail, have this perception too. For example, they compare their own bonuses to other colleagues' bonuses. These colleagues are people to whom they have a very close physical and cultural connection. They are not strangers and do not remain abstract like many other people whose existence is directly affected by the shuffling of billions.

We cannot keep our eyes shut forever because the countries of the world are growing closer together.

The closer we come together, the more the privileged will dread the poverty at their doorsteps. The walls will become higher and will be set with glass shards, the fences will become longer (the barrier between the

United States and Mexico now measures at least 700 miles in length), and we will have to stockpile military weapons.

Few people know, for example, that there is already a department in the EU, Frontex,[22] whose task it is to protect external borders from immigrants. They deploy warships whose crew force refugee boats to turn back, sometimes by confiscating stored water.[23] And anyone who lands at Bombay airport at night and takes a taxi into the financial district of the city cannot help but notice the countless homeless who line the streets for miles. Unless he pulls closed the curtains inside the limousine.

The world is becoming increasingly overcrowded, and it is only a question of time: How long can we allow ourselves to be unfair to the less developed countries and their citizens? This is one side.

The other is: We should not be unfair to ourselves. Because even though personhood itself connects us to all other people, there are still violent historical differences that have developed between nations and their unique economic development and traditions. It doesn't make sense, therefore, to expect the world to change according to our taste and understanding of justice and democracy. That would be abolishing the distinctions that exist among us, or even worse, it would be a cocktail of political proselytizing and colonialism.

So what can we do that won't involve exporting our arrogance or taking anything away from anyone?

We can take a chance, wait humbly and observe what develops. We can make sure that the clockwork of the economy ticks correctly and fairly. Every nation, every group of people has to find its own way to implement this fairness within its borders.

We have to create fair basic world conditions, but we should not make this depend on compliance to politics. And we should not take anything away from anyone in the world. Otherwise, this model of fairness will not be accepted.

I will describe the way this can be carried out in the next chapter, "Land – The Fair Distribution of Real Estate and a Worldwide Unconditional Income."

How quickly and closely the world is growing together can be easily seen in transnational social networks like Facebook. Since the sixties, there has also been the so-called "six degrees of separation" theory and the "small world experiment."[24] The theory is that any person can be connected to any other person on the planet by six acquaintances at most.

We should therefore very carefully consider what we expect of our neighbors or of fellow humans who are somewhat farther away. It will come back to us, in spite of whatever walls, fences, or security measures we put into place. The more mobile and globalized we become in the developed countries, the more we inevitably come closer to the rest of the world.

Even today personal security is an illusion. It is not true that terrorism stems from political or religious motives, like politicians would like to have us believe. Terrorism is nothing more than a slight jolt to the wall with which we protect alleged property and borrowed wealth. It is a taste of what is to come if we do not begin to treat each other fairly.

Fear of Change

When you acknowledge that everything changes
Then you won't hold onto anything.[25]

Laotse
(Chinese philosopher, 6th century BCE)

When we think about fairness in the world, alongside the feeling that it would be just, most of us experience a creeping, subtle fear. It disguises itself in the form of existential angst, ecology, and racist prejudices. The phrases that come from a desire to protect our vested interests "If all the Chinese drove cars, then pollution would increase even more quickly" or "We already had high unemployment rates and then a whole army of Indian engineers showed up in our country" or even the barbarically racist "There are certain races that don't have genes for working and are going to live off the hard-working people in this country."

All these fears are the result of prejudices and have no basis in reality, but all the same they are the material from which our thoughts and behavior grow. They are seldom challenged and it seems as though they have become the popular consensus. Otherwise there would be more outrage against statements like those made by Dr. Gerhard Schwarz, the departmental manager of economics for the Neue Zürcher Zeitung: *"All liberals in the world are of the opinion that borders should be open: for goods, for money, for services. It is becoming increasingly difficult when it comes to immigration, since one must consider whether one should charge admission of some kind, just like one charges admission at a club."*[26]

It is understandable to be afraid of people from foreign countries who want a share of our wealth. This fear comes from the misconception that people from underdeveloped countries will remain poor. It starts there – that there is not enough for everyone and that, therefore, at some point we will be competing for resources.

It is not necessarily so. As you will see in the following chapter, there is more than enough for everyone. Therefore, the fears that come from wanting to protect our vested interests are nothing but a misconception. They are human. However, they disappear immediately if we allow ourselves to form new thought patterns and to think outside of our habitual tendencies.

Despite all this, residual fear will remain – the fear that accompanies every change from what we know to something new. It is the apprehension of the unforeseeable, inherent in future events. All the same, we should fear not changing more than changing, since even if we overcome this crisis, new crises will still come to pass.

The biggest challenge lies in the trying to reconcile the differences between the "haves" and the "have-nots." The "haves" are all the people living in developed countries, whether they be celebrities, managers, welfare recipients, fund managers, or anti-globalization activists. Even the poor in these countries own more than the Indian migrant workers described in the introduction. Most importantly, however, we have largely the same chances of survival even if there are significant differences when it comes to our levels of education and inherited wealth. I don't mean that the developed countries are perfectly just and that they offer equal opportunities for all. We are still far away from that. However, with the work and social services these countries are usually able to provide, the probability of starving is very low.

Our fear of change does not come from basic fear of survival. It originates in our insufficient ability to imagine that there will be enough for everyone. I emphasize this so often because it represents the root of the whole problem: It is a problem with perspective, based on the two hearts that beat in our chests – greed and fairness. As soon as we look at these challenges from an economic point of view, we will acknowledge that the new construction of our economic clock poses no great economic problem.

3   The Fair Distribution of Real Estate and a Worldwide Unconditional Income

At the end of the seventies, the FAO (Food and Agriculture Organization of the United Nations) established the World Conference on Agrarian Reform and Rural Development, which unfortunately could not live up to its task.

Today land reforms are on the task lists of many developing countries.

Land reforms are defined as changes in the institutional arrangement of land use and land ownership as well as redistribution of agricultural assets, executed by the ruling party, in order to negotiate economic and political inconsistencies and conflicts without changing the dominant social structures and networks.[27]

The distribution of land and of natural and mineral resources is one of the greatest injustices and is a massive impediment to sustainable economic and ecological development. Only if we solve this problem can we approach distributive justice. Only if everyone has an equal share of the world's resources and the profits created from their use does the possibility of lasting peace exist.

In this chapter, I will introduce a model that distributes the existing wealth and taps available resources without creating losses for their current owners.

Who Owns the World?

*I as lawgiver lay it down that neither you yourself
nor your property belongs to you,
but that they belong to entire your family both past and future.*[28]

Plato
(Greek philosopher, 428- 348 BCE)

Consider your life, for a moment, as a gift. Think of your body, your experiences, and perceptions as loans, as things that disappear irretrievably with death. There is nothing that you can take with you, whether you believe in reincarnation, heaven and hell, or in another form of life after death.

During your journey through life, you probably think about the inevitability of death very seldom. Most of your actions are based on the idea of things going on forever. However, at some point sickness and death will catch up with you. You will die and leave everything behind you.

Though it is so large, you share this planet with about six and a half billion other people, and every day their numbers increase.

Who owns this earth and its treasures? Who owns this planet on which you spend your borrowed time?

If you are lucky, you were born in a developed region in the northern hemisphere. You do not know hunger and you live in a country with a stable legal system. You're doing well.

Of course, as an informed person you have heard of injustice in the world and you know about distribution conflicts, hunger, and pain on the other side of the globe. You also have the notion that everything is somehow connected, though the direct connection to you and your life and wealth is often difficult to fathom.

Imagine that you own a home, a condominium or even just a small piece of land. You saved money and bought it as provision for your old age. It is not speculation and is nothing special.

How did you acquire this property? How was it possible for you to purchase it?

You are probably saying, "I bought it" or "I inherited it" and with this answer you expect to satisfy all further questions.

But from whom did you buy it?

You answer, "From the previous owner" or "From the local authorities that designated it as land for building".

How did the land end up in the hands of the previous owner or of the local authorities? Is it really possible to buy and sell land?

"Of course people in the developed countries can buy land," you will say. You would be forgetting, however, that the idea of ownership of land is not very old. Until not too long ago, land in most countries belonged to the rulers of each respective territory. Ownership included everything that existed on the land: people, animals, buildings, and natural resources. This time is known as feudalism.

But who owned the land before a ruler set his fence posts into the ground? It was available, that is clear, but who owned it? There was no land registry at the time.

If you really consider it, it will dawn on you: No one owns the land, and at the same time, everyone does.

Before people settled, before they adopted feudal systems, they were nomads. After that, people first began cultivating the land, and ownership of land had no meaning. There were also no borders. How else could modern people, who originated in Africa, have spread out over the whole world?

The appropriation of land is a bloodstained story. A few people at some point began to set posts into the ground, which upset other people, and thus the first warlike contention came about.

In order to understand this in historical terms, we can look at the history of North America. Before settlers from Europe arrived, the land belonged to the Native Americans: the prairies and forests, giant herds of buffalo – untouched nature with few signs of human intrusion. Most indigenous people lived as nomads without land ownership. Promptly after landing, the first settlers began to indiscriminately appropriate what seemed to them to be vast tracts of unclaimed land. Anyone who knows this story knows that the Native Americans were almost wiped out because the settlers were the stronger group; in this battle the law of superior strength and superior weapons was what counted.

It is interesting that most of these settlers were not land owners themselves in the countries from which they emigrated. Among them were many Irish and Scottish farmers who left when their feudal lords decided that it made more sense economically to raise sheep than to grow basic crops. When these "have-nots" landed in the new world, they saw no other option than to simply take the land for themselves.

Similar things have happened in every country: settlers, dictators, and nations all seize land. It is an indiscriminate practice and follows no law.

Ownership and inheritance emerged as legal notions so that a person could appropriate land, keep it for generations, and pass it on without having to fight over its borders every time. Authorities like the land registry, which certified the appropriation of land, were introduced along with inheritance law.

Both property law and inheritance law are philosophically questionable constructions. They legalize a world that is divided according to the laws of stronger social groups, a world that is contrary to every sense of justice and extend this arbitrariness past their own deaths onto following generations.

Concretely, this means that even the small pieces of land that you may own were at some point taken, without reason, from the global community and set into private ownership.

To say that ownership of any piece of land was simply introduced when national institutions registered it with their land registry offices is to ignore the violent facts of history. It seems as if it were always this way, as if ownership and property were the most natural things in the world, as if real estate was an economic product like apples or bananas, something that the current owner had made an effort to produce. If we look closely however, we will see that owned land is nothing more than stolen property since it was taken by means of thievery, force, and, with no great infrequency, murder.

No one wants to know anything about that today, so we rely on property law, on offices that register borders, and on the fact that we paid a specific price. Apart from quarreling among neighbors, everything seems to be honest and fair.

You would be right in this supposition – no injustice was committed in your world. You bought land, you paid for it. The injustice lies a hundred years in the past, and at some point, one has to shut the book of history. Things are how they are, and that's good.

Does something in you rise in outrage at the mention of these thoughts?

That is the fear that someone will take away your legally acquired land and force you off of it. Let me be perfectly clear: No one is going to take anything away from you; this vision could not work that way. No one wants your house or land. Allow yourself to consider these thoughts even if you are trembling with fear of your property being seized. I assure you, in the end you will be wealthier than before. Before it's too late, you should at least contemplate these thoughts: in the distant past, the ground that your house sits upon was taken into ownership completely arbitrarily.

And perhaps you can also allow yourself to ponder this question: Who owned this world with its great expanses, its oceans, all its natural resources and unique wildlife before it was appropriated?

The French philosopher Jean-Jacques Rousseau (1712-1778) once declared, *"There is in the depth of souls an innate principle of justice according to which, in spite of our own maxims, we judge our actions and those of others to be good or bad. And it is to this principle that I give the name conscience."*[29]

By the principle of justice, no one can own the world other than its inhabitants, the six and a half billion people who live on and from it.

No more and no fewer.

If we use the principle of justice, it belongs as much to Osama bin Laden as to George W. Bush. It belongs to the people on death row as much as to their executioners. It belongs to a baby just as it belongs to an old man, to both men and to women. It belongs to everyone equally.

People who want to disavow this fact or contradict it must ask themselves what they are imposing on others and whether they have lost their sense of fairness and their consciences.

Sharing without Losing

*To relinquish part of your own property, to give up your rights –
creates happiness if it shows great wealth.
This is called generosity.*[30]

Friedrich Nietzsche
(German philosopher, 1844-1900)

Maybe you own a house or several acres of land. Other people own
oil fields, still others own freshwater springs, a few own diamond mines,
and the white house in Washington, D.C. belongs to the American people
and is held in trust by the current administration. This is official and has
been noted by the proper authorities.

Now let's think about justice. Can we condemn these people right
away? Should any one person or institution take away their assets and distribute them to other people?

They worked hard and honestly to buy their property. If they did
not buy it and just took it, they still put in fences to mark the boundaries.
Furthermore, they invested in it – they made the land useful or bored holes
to reach its natural resources.

It is perfectly illusionistic to think that someone should simply give
up their land, and expropriation, a compulsory transfer to public property,
in no way corresponds to general feelings of justice and fairness.

How could the world community attain land in a way that allowed
everyone to have part of it: the current owners and the people who do not
own any land? How can the world and its resources be shared fairly, without anyone losing anything?

Imagine a *World Authority for Currency and Land.* A combination of a
national bank and a discretionary real estate administration on an international level. Maybe this authority would exist under the United Nations, the
World Bank, or the International Monetary Fund.

This agency would buy all property and land from their current owners. This would also include undistributed and undeveloped land; it includes all land and all oceans worldwide, regardless of how they are being
used.

The World Authority for Currency and Land would pay for these things based on their current market values. For a plot of land in the desert, the price might be very low and for one with an oil field underneath, very high. Market values, after all, include not yet extracted oil – they include the price of the raw materials we know to be under the earth.

The price for all the plots of land in the whole world may be enormous, and you will ask yourself where all this money comes from. I will address this question in the chapter "Money and Why it Only Works if We Believe in It." Until then, assume that the World Authority for Currency and Land has the necessary capital at hand.

Next, you are probably asking yourself: Why should I sell my house or my land? In the end I would probably have to move out and maybe even lose my livelihood!

None of this would happen since it would not be just, and I have promised you a fair economic system – a new economy where no one loses.

The moment you sold your property to the World Authority for Currency and Land and received your payment, you would be able to continue to use your property if you paid a lease. The World Authority for Currency and Land would offer you a lifetime lease contract or, if you are a company, perhaps a lease contract for the duration of the average world life expectancy. Over the duration of the contract, your total lease payments would be less than the amount you received for your land. So by selling your land you would make a decent profit. In this transaction, worldwide wealth would not be distributed in a new way, nor would the rights of use for land and oceans change.

This process is nothing new. It has been done by companies for many years. It is known as "sale and leaseback"[31] and is a special type of lease. An organization sells a piece of real estate to a leasing company and then leases it back in order to keep using the property. For the initial organization, this process is like receiving a loan. It is quite an ordinary way to raise capital. But it is also beneficial to the leasing company as they also earn a significant sum. The process has even been established across international borders where it is known as "cross-border leasing."[32]

Now, the property owners would not sell to a dubious leasing company that wants to make as much money as possible from this transaction. On the contrary, they would sell to the highly respected World Authority for Currency and Land, an institution that belongs to all people and that has no interest in making a profit from this transaction.

Rest assured that nothing would change with the sale of your property: You would inhabit it, you would cultivate your land, extract and sell the raw materials under the ground.

There is only one restriction: You would not be allowed to lease the property you yourself are leasing. Only the World Authority for Currency and Land would be able to administer the right to use the property. This restriction would prevent wealthy people from leasing large pieces of land in order to make a profit by subleasing or subletting them to the less wealthy. This is not a regulation that would affect homeowners. Instead, it is a protection against speculating with property that belongs to all citizens of the world.

What would happen after you died or when the lease contract ran out?

Then the World Authority for Currency and Land would invite tenders to bid on the property that you used during your lifetime and would award a new contract to the highest bidder. Of course your heirs (or in the case of a company, the company) would have leasehold rights as long as their bid lay within reasonable limits. However, the World Authority for Currency and Land would have to pay attention to market-driven bids, since the lease income would indebt it to all world citizens.

And if someone absolutely does not want to sell whether the bid was fair or not?

That would only apply to individuals. With the sale of their property, companies would receive an enormous capital sum. Liquidity is the most important thing for new investments that might be required, for example, in order extracting oil or diamonds from the earth more quickly or in greater quantities. From an entrepreneurial perspective, the refusal to sell property would be silly, particularly if others were making a significant profit doing so.

Companies that did not sell would eventually register bankruptcy since soon they would no longer have the financial means with which to compete with their rivals. Just a small change in bankruptcy law would be required in order for the World Authority for Currency and Land to give the land to a creditor in exchange for a payment.

Real estate firms present one exception. Their business model would be made irrelevant and they would have to look for a new field of work.

Since they would receive a large sum of money for their property, it should not be difficult for them to develop new business ideas.

For most part, it would be individuals who would not want to sell. Of course no one can be forced to do something for their whole lives. After such a person passes away however, as is the case with bankruptcy, all property could go to the World Authority for Currency and Land. The person's heirs would of course receive an appropriate compensation. So all problems would be solved. With enough political will, it would take three or four generations at most for private property to cease to exist completely.

Sharing with Profit

*Injustice anywhere
threatens justice everywhere.*[33]

Martin Luther King
(American theologian and civil-rights activist, 1929-1968)

Is the world fairer now?

No. The landowners remain landowners and the wealth is not distributed more fairly.

However, we have not yet spoken about the World Authority for Currency and Land's lease income, about how that income would be distributed. There can be only one principle to guide this distribution: "One person, one vote."[34] After deducting its administrative costs, the World Authority for Currency and Land would distribute all lease income to all citizens of the world. And it would mean that an American receives exactly as much as an Indian, a Berliner exactly as much as man living in the African countryside.

Thus, the World Authority for Currency and Land's lease income allows for a *worldwide unconditional basic income.*

However, this income would not be quite enough for citizens in the developed countries to live on. Therefore, what could be distributed would not suffice.

This is not important, however. It is much more meaningful that of the six and a half billion people on the earth, about five billion have a purchasing power of less than 600 US dollars per month, and of those, three and a half billion have less than 300 US dollars a month. The poorest of the poor have a purchasing power of 50 US dollars a month or less.

Therefore, an additional 50 US dollars or less per month could significantly increase purchasing power in the less developed countries.

Be careful not to confuse purchasing power – or, to be more precise, purchasing power parity – with income. In the less developed countries, the latter is usually considerably less than purchasing power. In India, for example, a one-dollar bill (1 USD) has a purchasing power of 4.50 USD. That means for 1 USD you can buy 4.50 USD worth of goods. In comparison, a one-dollar bill in Switzerland has a purchasing power of only 0.60 USD.[35] Therefore, the poor would receive considerably more purchasing power than is received for the lease contracts.

What would people do with this sudden sum of money?

Maybe you would also lease land from the World Authority for Currency and Land and buy a hoe or plow. Maybe you would buy goods for your daily needs.

Don't forget that the money would be equally distributed among all citizens of the world. Its biggest effect would be revealed in its distribution to those who previously had the least – the poorest of the poor.

It is necessary to assume that worldwide unconditional basic income would end up where it belonged – with all the citizens of the world. This would pose no great problems in developed countries, even if a greedy company kept a significant sum for itself. But what would happen in the countries that are governed by dictators? What would happen in really corrupt systems, where African potentates or wealthy Saudi Arabian families will fill their own pockets at the others' expense? Or in countries like China, where one party believes itself to be all knowing and to be able to rule over its citizens completely?

These are difficulties that cannot be solved from the outside or by an intervention by the international community.

All the interventions that the international community has made in recent years – in the Balkans, in Iraq and Afghanistan – have shown that these actions from the outside quite possibly do more harm than good. Sustainable changes in society have to be processes that come from within, as was shown in the removal of the last European dictators in Portugal, Spain, and Greece, and in the collapses of both East Germany and the Soviet Union.

It sounds so callous to say that citizens have to provide distributive justice within their respective countries, and in some cases even have to run the risk of rebelling or revolting.

The only thing the rest of the world could do to support them would be to provide information about the World Authority for Currency and Land and its worldwide unconditional basic income, to which every person would be entitled. This should be unfiltered information that incites a revolution as fast as possible and whose progress entails that despots would be hunted down in the deserts or in the outback.

"That sounds good," most readers will say. But wouldn't international corporations maintain the same interests in this situation that they have today? And, in the implementation of their global interests, wouldn't they be supported by the same greedy governments in developed countries? Why should the motto "What's good for America is good for the world" suddenly change? Why shouldn't corrupt regimes continue to be supported and supplied with weapons as long as they delivery cheap raw materials? Why should we trouble ourselves with whether or not every citizen receives this worldwide unconditional basic income?

On an economic level, the answer is simple: because it would be in the best interest of global companies and developed nations.

The negative outcomes that would arise if every citizen did *not* receive a worldwide unconditional basic income are apparent even today and cost industrial countries billions.

The problem is not the money that flows into countries as foreign aid – this is peanuts. It is the costs for trade barriers, protective duties, and border security. It is the expenditure for fences and walls that are meant to prevent the people in developing countries from coming to us. It is all the costs that arise from trying to keep the poor and needy out in order to continue to make a profit from them.

Whether the Worldwide Unconditional Basic Income Will End Up Where it Belongs

*Henry Ford once said, he had to pay his workers a reasonable
amount so that they would be able to buy his cars.
If the world economy doesn't recover,
the export countries won't even be able to sell their goods.[36]*

Dominique Strauss-Kahn
(IMF Managing Director und former French Finance and Economy
Minister, born 1949)

Would you emigrate if, in the place where you live, your purchasing
power were more than doubled in a single day? Would you a risk an ardu-
ous escape over barbed wire and across the ocean with a relatively low
chance of survival, if you had the means with which to establish a life where
you already live? Would you flee if you knew that, in the place where you
were going, your purchasing power was worth significantly less?

No.

You would try to use what you had to buy land and a hoe or tractor.
Maybe you would open a small shop or a restaurant with two plastic chairs.
If you have children, you would of course also spend part of your money
on their education. Or maybe you would only invest in your modest home,
maybe you would buy a television.

What you would definitely not do is go to a place where you have
nothing but your body and your labor to sell, a place where your money and
your purchasing power are worth nothing.

The assumption is, of course, that the worldwide unconditional basic
income would end up where it belonged, that you would not be cheated.

Why should global corporations care whether or not you receive
your portion of the money? Don't they make a living by selling raw materials from less developed countries and exploiting their cheap labor?

You're right, but only at first glance.

If you look closely, you will see that global corporations make a living not only from cheap raw materials – produced at the cost of sweat and
blood – but also from the refining processes and the marketable products

that are created from those materials. Profit and value are created in the transformation of the raw materials into products. Coffee beans, for example, are not only grown and harvested, but also dried, roasted, and packed as ground coffee. In almost the same manner ore is mined, and steel and then weapons or surgical instruments are manufactured.

Products require a market. They require consumers.

Markets in the developed countries are, for the most part, saturated. They carry almost everything that is necessary in life. The biggest costs associated with consumable products are marketing and advertisement, whose purpose is to make new products seem appealing to people so that they will want to buy them. On the other hand, the situation in developing countries is completely different. There, much of what we take for granted is still needed.

However, the populations of these countries had almost no purchasing power before the worldwide unconditional basic income and therefore commanded no interest from global corporations. If this changed, even just a little, the multi-national companies would wait in line for their business.

India is an example of this situation. In the last few years, India has quickly changed from being a developing nation to an emerging market whose middleclass is composed of over 320 million potential customers. Purchasing power in India is still low but it is growing steadily and will surpass the United States in the next ten to twenty years. This is assuming, of course, that the country does not plunge into a civil war because of social unrest.

Since this is purely an economic consideration, let's look at the numbers: There are six and a half billion people in the world. About five billion people have less than 600 USD per month in purchasing power, and of those, three and a half billion people have less than 300 USD per month in purchasing power.

Now, every person would receive an unconditional basic income in addition to their existing purchasing power.

In the developed countries, this would be too little to create many new developments. The lower the purchasing power, however, the greater the effect unconditional basic income would have. There would definitely be regions in which purchasing power more than doubled. Corporations and business people who did not take advantage of this potential would be going against their own best interests.

Only in terms of a global economic system would the money end up where it belonged – in the hands of the poorest of the poor.

You can argue that a dictator who pockets the money for himself would be increasing his own purchasing power. That is correct. However, sustainable profit is not created from luxury goods like yachts and champagne, but from goods associated with daily needs like plastic containers and cooking pots. Also, it is important for every global corporation to have many customers – many customers who need completely ordinary things. That is where money is made.

As you can clearly see, in my vision I leave a fair economic system to the regulators of the market and am far from an abolishment of capitalism or of a global economy.

Of course it would take time for such a system to grow roots. Many great efforts would have to be made before the last person in a remote village receives his unconditional basic income and it would probably take generations before the last dictators in the world were gone. All the same, when distributed fairly, the proceeds created from the leasing of property and resources would create long-term, sustainable, life-promoting conditions on this planet, from which no one can emigrate.

The Realization – Justice and Force

Justice without force is powerless; force without justice is tyrannical.
Justice without force will be thwarted, as long as wicked men exist;
force without justice will be reprobated by all the good.
Therefore, justice and force must be joined, in order that
what is just may be powerful, and that what is powerful may be
just.[37]

Blaise Pascal
(French mathematician, physicist, and philosopher, 1623-1662)

The biggest objection to the implementation of such a reform is that there will always be people who find loopholes and use them, fraudulently, to their own advantage.

Many people will first think of multinational corporations, the Mafia, corrupt governments, drug and weapon dealers, and banks. The possibility that rules and laws will not be followed is one that always exists. It cannot be avoided.

But the World Authority for Currency and Land's rules would not be broken on such a large scale. On the contrary, it would happen mostly in cases of emergency and ignorance. It would be in companies' best interests to participate in the new economic system, as I have already discussed, and few would have any objection whatsoever. All the same, as the introductory quote by Pascal makes clear, this plan needs to be enforced in order to make sure it is implemented.

Opposition to this new system will come, first and foremost, from places where the population is dependent on settling, fire clearing, and using the land for short-term production by stripping it of its fertile soil. There are places, like the Amazon for instance, where sustainable cultivation of the land was previously not desired.

Also, there would be conflicts in some areas in which people were used to simply taking without having a lease contract. This includes illegal logging and fishing, whose perpetrators do not pay attention to borders but hide behind the term "international waters".

The technology for uncovering violations like illegal seizure of land or production from the sea already exists: There is a satellite system that orbits Earth. It has done well in field tests and is currently being used primarily for the military's espionage.

But in most cases, education would be much more useful than an army. Military force has done little to help poor farmers who do not own land. These farmers lack knowledge about sustainable agriculture and urgently need food to survive, so they repeatedly take land and, after a short time, leave it behind, depleted of it resources. In all of these cases, programs for education and development would be needed to help people learn to be economical and profitable with the wealth they received from the World Authority for Currency and Land. Such programs could be realized most easily if the World Authority for Currency and Land combined the proceeds from poor farmers' lease contracts with corresponding programs to help them. Only then could unconditional basic income turn into working capital. Only then would the holders of that capital find themselves in positions in which they did not have to worry about hunger or income.

On the other hand, the World Authority for Currency and Land should not be a "toothless tiger". If it puts under special protection certain regions or resources that serve everyone, like tropical rainforests, particular areas of the ocean, or drinking water access, then it should also be able to implement its guidelines in terms of the international community. Here, well-intentioned reprimands would not be enough.

Further opposition to unconditional basic income may be raised with regard to ecology. After all, what would people do with their purchasing power? They would squander it on things they don't really need – cars, refrigerators, air-conditioners, televisions – and the environment would pay the price with all the pollution created.

This is another threat to our small, peaceful developed world. This time, however, the threat does not come from people who want to come to our country, against whose rushing we build walls, but by the pollution that these people leave behind. Fences and armed border patrols cannot help combat poisonous fumes and global CO_2 emissions.

An argument like this may seem plausible to many people. It is in fact not only cynical, but also wrong.

People would buy more products, that is the point of this hypothetical situation. Purchasing power and consumption worldwide would increase so that eventually, no one would starve. Over a longer period of time, the conditions would begin to harmonize. Each citizen should have a minimum amount of basic goods at his or her disposal, and there should be equally accessible wealth – though probably modest at first – for all.

In regard to these goods and the circumstances by which they are produced and disposed of: Who says that this general prosperity can't be ecological? Who says that there wouldn't be interest in ecological sustainability once basic needs are fullfilled? Was it any different here in the developed countries?

No.

"Eating comes first, then morals,"[38] wrote Bertolt Brecht in *The Threepenny Opera*. However, that doesn't mean that we have to abandon the insights we have today, and it doesn't mean that the less developed countries will automatically make the same mistakes we made. It simply means: As long as one person in this world is starving, it is cynical to prohibit his satiation on the basis of ecological arguments.

Moreover, who says that companies that received a significant cash inflow by selling their property to the World Authority for Currency and Land wouldn't want to tailor their products to an increasingly sophisticated and ecologically aware client base? They would have to do something with the capital they received, otherwise they would just lose it.

Worldwide land reform and unconditional basic income are only one side of the coin. The other is monetary reform, a reform that would render both clinging to money and excessive speculation impossible. It would not reward the people who hoard money, but rather those who spend it and keep it flowing. You will see exactly how that would function in the chapter "Money and Why it Only Works If We Believe in It."

Don't underestimate corporations' motivation to invest their money in new products if the old and ecologically outdated ones are no longer profitable.

The Outcome and Why it is so Difficult for Us to Say Goodbye to Colonialism

*There are know-it-alls who never comprehend
that one can be right and still be an idiot.*[39]

Martin Kessel
(German writer, 1901-1990)

Most people's biggest fear will involve the enormous sum of money needed to purchase all property and the daunting task of distributing the lease income. This comes from people's apprehension that, if everyone suddenly has so much money, worldwide inflation and drastic price increases will occur.

Stay calm. The total worldwide unconditional basic income would be far less than the amount that circulates around the globe as speculation money. Moreover, it is connected to the value of all property and that property's respective lease income. It cannot, therefore, grow illimitably like virtual money that speculators and gamblers play with. It cannot form the kind of huge bubble which, if popped, would endanger us all.

The basic income funds would be similar to the gold standard since they would be based on the existing property in the world, a limited asset. Also, as long as the population increases by about 203,000 people per day (1.14 % per year),[40] there would be no increase in the unconditional basic income per person. Instead, until around the year 2050, monthly payments would decrease in order to settle at a median value.

It is a fact: The more people who live on this planet, the more parts the lease income would have to be divied.

Returning to people's fear of inflation. Inflation is a spiral of simultaneously or slightly deferred increasing prices and salaries. Inflation only occurs when both increase together. The worldwide unconditional basic income could not increase on short notice since the lease contracts are based on long term agreements.

What would definitely occur would be a price increase of certain products. The first group would be products that, in less developed countries, would suddenly come into demand and create bottlenecking in the current delivery and transport systems, because for example the manufacturer cannot build a factory nearby very quickly. This price increase would be temporary in nature. With decreasing demand and with the construction of supply chains, prices would settle down again.

The second group of products – the prices of which would increase to some degree and permanently stay higher than they are now – are goods whose raw materials come from developing countries or whose manufacturing processes are completed there. It's obvious: A worker who receives an unconditional basic income would no longer be subject to working for much less money. There would no longer be African cotton pickers or Chinese industrial workers who toil away for one U.S. dollar a day or less. That means that the price for a t-shirt at a discount clothing store would increase. To keep the price from exploding, it would have to be artificially be held up momentarily through trade restrictions, protective duties, and subsidies that would protect native producers or national populations from cheap competition in the developing countries.

True globalization, truly fair competition between different countries does not exist even if politicians, unionists, and anti-globalization activists would like us to believe the opposite.

Worldwide unconditional basic income would solve this problem since protective duties and trade barriers against cheap competition would be required. The products and services would maintain their prices, and the market to which global, free business belongs could then function again.

Now, everyone in the whole world should be happy about this adjustment to wages, even if it is a minimal one. But that would not be the case. On the contrary, there would be a great uproar about job security in the developed countries and labor leaders would reveal their true faces, their protection of acquired possession. But I have consolation for them too: It would not be worse than it already is. Of course the markets would shift, and of course new production centers would be constructed in the less developed countries. However, since wages would be adjusted over a few generations, this would not lead to a world economic crisis or mass layoffs. These crises are not caused by the emergence of new markets but by the loss of internal buyers. They do not come about as long as people spend money freely, only when people hoard it fearfully.

Another point that I would like to address and that some might bring into debate: Why should there be unconditional worldwide basic income for everyone? Why not put all the money into social projects, into development aid, education, medical care, and general improvement of the state of welfare?

The answer is: because it would give people individual responsibility and dignity. Dignity to survive by means of modest seed capital and one's own labor. Dignity to lead an independent, free life. A life in which each person can decide whether he buys a plough and works or lies in the sun for a year.

At this point, the know-it-all will come running with his colonial ideas: "How are people supposed to know what's good and sustainable? They have no experience and would be swindled out of their money in the end!"

If we want the model to work, we should set aside our presumptions and take an open-minded look at the world. We would have to learn that our model of social standards and democracy does not apply in every situation and would have to accept that there are many different cultural approaches that are equal to our science- and reason-based approach: Muslim, Hindu, creationist, and many more. And every individual and every country would have the freedom to decide for themselves – without outside intervention.

It follows that one consequence of the implementation of the unconditional worldwide basic income would be that the know-it-alls from the developed countries would lose influence. It might be difficult for us to get rid of them. The market and the parties involved can regulate everything else by themselves.

In order for a fair economic system to be successful outside the third world, to work for the benefit of everyone, in addition to property reform and unconditional worldwide basic income, a monetary reform would be required. It would require a currency that would benefit everyone without taking anything away from anyone else, without reducing existing wealth.

I will describe the way this currency would work in the next chapter.

Here, once again, is a short summary of the property reform and the unconditional worldwide basic income: A newly founded authority would buy all land. This agency would pay the current market value or a reasonable price based on the natural resources available, the so-called expected value. All property including the oceans – the total surface area of the earth – would then belong to this authority. In the next step, the world authority would lease the land back to the previous owners, and all income from the lease contracts would be equally divided among the six and a half billion people as *unconditional basic income*. That way, every person on the planet would be an owner of the world to an equal degree, and the *World Authority for Currency and Land* would act as a trustee for these assets. No one would be forced to give up their property, no one would be poor. Everyone would get an equal piece of the pie.

Ideally, this vision's effects would be global. It could, however, also be applied locally in crisis regions as so-called "nation-building."[i]

To clarify this, I would like to take Iraq – destroyed by both war and civil war – as an example. The country is multiethnic, composed of different religious and ethnic groups. Every one of these groups mistrusts the others. Robbery, murder, and territorial conflicts are part of everyday life. On the other hand, the country possesses enormous oil resources, and if those resources were fairly distributed, all citizens could partake of the wealth. Applied to Iraq, the described model of fair distribution would not immediately eliminate all the reservations the different groups have about one another, but it would create room for negotiations among the groups and for a government that would represent everyone. All of the tensions that stand in the way of distributive justice would be released.

---

[i] Nation-building refers to the process of constructing or structuring a national identity using the power of the state. This process aims at the unification of the people or peoples within the state so that it remains politically stable and viable in the long run. Nation-building can involve the use of propaganda or major infrastructure development to foster social harmony and economic growth. From http://en.wikipedia.org/wiki/Nation-building.

4   Money and Why it Only Works
if We Believe in It

Capitalism is based on the strange conviction
that horrible people with horrible motives somehow manage
to make a positive contribution to the common good.[41]

John Maynard Keynes
(British economist, politician, and mathematician, 1883–1946)

Money was invented as a general means of exchange and payment for goods and services. Its most prominent and most dangerous qualities that differentiate it from goods and services are: Money cannot go bad, and has no storage costs. According to economic conditions, this will cause a money holder to save and hoard his money, or to speculate with it in the expectation of good profits.

This leads to a situation where in times of economic boom, money floods the globe in seconds flat; while in bad times it stays in vaults and in accounts and is absent from international financial circulation. At the moment times are bad, and though there is much too much money in existence, it leaves most banks and companies very slowly. In such a situation, most countries try to keep their economies afloat with economic stimulus plans and subsidies. The result is that billions of dollars are flooded into the already existent money on the market. The more that the total money supply increases, the more likely it is that there will be another, even larger crisis.

In this chapter, I will describe how the money supply and financial crises are related, as well as why people are able to speculate with money. In addition, I will introduce a model in which there can always be enough money on the market without a need for state support even in bad times – a model that also allows the money supply, which has been far too swollen for generations, the cause of all crises, to finally equalize. An additional effect of this visionary model is an extensive reduction of speculative peaks, which would lead to a long-term elimination of the poverty they create.

Money from Nothing

The worst effect of capitalism is
that people believe
everything that they can pay for belongs to them.[42]

Martin Walser
(German author, born 1927)

One of the most frightening aspects of money is the fact that it only works as long as we believe in it. If the belief in money's value dissolved, through a loss of trust in the nation that produced it for example, money could lose its entire buying power overnight. This could happen faster than you would believe.

You probably think that something like that couldn't happen to the coins and bills in your wallet – you probably have a firm trust in your balance at the bank.

Try the following experiment, though: Draw some currency yourself, sign it on the back, and then try to buy something with it. At the counter, everyone will laugh in your face. Your hand-made money wouldn't even be worth as much as a bad joke.

What is it that distinguishes your money from the money that a central bank prints and issues?

Ok, a bank's money is made by means of an elaborate process, it looks better than your hand-made money, and is of course forgery-proof. Moreover, you've only made two or three bills, a central bank prints millions.

But aside from these technical discrepancies in production methods, what makes it so different? Why does the central bank's money achieve buying power while your hand-made money achieves only a weary laugh?

It is belief. The central bank is generally recognized and is considered trustworthy. You, on the other hand, are recognized by only the people who know you.

And what makes a central bank so trustworthy that everyone believes in the numbers they print on a colorful scrap of paper?

It is the promise that the numbers printed on a bill can buy goods of exactly that value, or that the money can be exchanged for other currencies. However, this promise and the belief in it are illusory. There is much more money in the world than there are available material equivalents.

In short, this means: If all of the citizens of a country suddenly wanted to exchange all of their money – their cash and their accounts – for goods, the central bank's promise would collapse like a house of cards. All of that carefully manufactured money would be worth no more than your hand-made bills.

An example: All the saving deposits in Germany constitute a total of about 4.5 trillion euros. I'm speaking here only about savings accounts, not about securities, life insurance, and things like that. In 2008 however, the gross national product, the income of the entire country, was only about 2.4 trillion euros. The chancellor can keep assuring Germans that their savings are secure, but mathematically it doesn't work out. There is a similar situation in every country, which is why reasonable countries have abstained from a guaranteed protection of assets from the beginning.

You don't want to believe it and would like an explanation of why it is that way?

According to monetary theory, all the money in circulation – cash and accounts – should correspond exactly to the amount of goods and services that are available on the market. If not by gold, as was the case in the past, money should at least be backed by the sum of available goods. That means that there should be only as much money as there are services, goods, and real estate – in short, things that can be bought.[i]

This is logical because money has no value in and of itself. It is and remains a printed bill or a number on your account statement. Its value must be based on something.

Indeed, these fundamentals of monetary theory have not applied for a long time – if they did then there would be no large problems or crises in the global financial system. Money would have its value – a different one in

---

[i] By the money supply in circulation, the so-called money supply aggregate M3 is meant. The US Central Bank Fed defines M3 as the following: all US dollar cash reserves in bills and coins plus current US dollar checking accounts plus all US dollar deposit certificates (for example government bonds) and all US dollar money market accounts (inc. Eurodollar reserves, transferable US dollar securities holdings and dollar foreign exchange holdings of most non-European countries).

developing countries than in industrial ones, but all the same it would be calculable and decidedly safe. Everything would be fine.

Why doesn't monetary theory work anymore?

It has to do with the fact that, for a long while now, we have been living above our means – "on credit" – we could no longer pay off our debts even if we wanted to.

The United States has the biggest debts. Following it are countries such as Japan, Germany, etc. and then come the developing countries. In a careless moment, all of these countries fired up their printing machines to make new money. They began to print more money than was backed by goods and services. I will explain to you why they did that, and why there was nothing else they could have done.

A country, a company, or a person wants to buy something, and there isn't enough money available at the moment. That country, company, or person assumes, however, that they will have that money in the future, and so go into debt.

For example, you want to buy a new car but at the moment you can't afford it. You hope that as soon as you have the car, you will be able to get a job that is farther away but better paid. You will then earn more money and could pay for the car later. But you need it now. So you go to your bank and borrow the money, and you use it to get the car. You take out a loan.

But where does the money for the car come from? You haven't earned it yet. Only later on you will sell your labor, and you will receive your salary even further in the future. Actually, the money you use to buy your car might not even be on the market yet.

The money comes from your bank, to which you are in debt. And your bank, in turn, has the money from the central bank that printed it.

You probably stop short now at the word "printed." But that is just where the problem lies, though in much larger dimensions than in the example of the car. A single car would be easy to deal with, but it's hundreds of thousands! And not just cars, but machines, houses, and much more.

Let's go further: It doesn't go as planned with your new job. You didn't get it. But now you have a car that you don't need and debts that you need even less. You're getting into a tight spot.

"No problem," says your bank, because the car has its own value. It was a new car, a little too big for you, but it has the latest technology and, most of all, it's a brand name that has lasting value. Even in three years it will still get a good price on the used car market. The bank then makes you an offer for a new loan with better conditions. You are still trustworthy: young, well-educated, without a criminal record, and childless.[i] The bank gives you money and maybe you buy a small, well situated condo to rent out because in the mean time you've been doing well.

Everyone believes in a golden future, you yourself most of all, and of course the bank. And the central bank that prints money believes in turn in your bank and that it only gives credit to clients who are financially secure.

It might go well for awhile and you could lead a relatively untroubled life – until the renter in your condo moves out and you can't find any new ones. And, in the used car market, your car doesn't sell for as much as you had hoped. No one wants to buy a gas guzzler because the price of oil has been driven up violently by a war in the Middle East. Now it's getting really tight and it's just a question of time until you become bankrupt.

It's not that way just for you. Recent years were good years, and many people believed that things would be on an eternal upswing. All of the numbers pointed to it too. But it didn't turn out that way, and now masses of people can't pay off their loans.

What should your bank do, then, if it doesn't want to be thrown into the maelstrom of bankruptcy? What should the central bank do, since it printed the money that your bank gave you?

It's no problem.

The central bank prints even more money and lends it to your local bank. Your bank makes you an offer to combine all of your old debts and give you a new loan with less interest. In the end, the economy has to function and you will only buy new things when you are at least reasonably happy and able to pay.

Your willingness to buy has consequences: As long as you are buying, the factories run at full speed and you have secure employment. And

---

[i] To equate having a criminal record with having children may seem cynical, but these are the exact terms used by many rating agencies for credit applications. Criminal records represent unreliability and children represent additional costs – both are classified by banks as large risks. Parents should not be outraged because they are in the same boat as all freelancers, that is doctors, architects, lawyers, writers, actors and many others.

as long as you have that, the bank can hope that one day you will pay off your debts.

So keep going; everything is back where it started.

The concept of keeping the market going by printing money was put into practice by Alan Greenspan,[43] the former Chairman of the American Federal Reserve. Since the mid-eighties, whenever there was a hiccup in the American economy, many millions of new dollars were printed and pumped into the market. And because America is the leading economic nation and everyone wants to do business with it, many countries chose, or were forced, to imitate this practice.

Now it is not only about so-called consumer and mortgage credit, i.e. debt for cars or real estate. The United States has been applying the practice of printing money to gain buying power for many years, for instance to pay its bills for crude oil and for all of its wars since Vietnam. As long as most other countries believe in the dollar and are dependant on it, that practice will work, too. However, with every crisis where money is printed to support the economy, as is currently being done for banks and insurance companies, the volume of money increases. And with every crisis, the amounts that are necessary for this support increase.

It is an unending spiral.

One that doesn't really add up. At some point the time comes when the central bank's money garners just as little trust as your hand-made money. This situation occurs when the international financial community stops trusting the country to which the central bank belongs. That country's money is then no longer valuable outside of its own borders, and its business with other countries collapses. As a result, even within their own country, people start losing trust in their central bank's money, and after a short time no one trusts its value anymore. Many developing countries were in this position after printing too much money – at the end of 2008, so was Iceland. Other countries that continued printing money, for example the United States, are still trusted only by force of the fact that the world economy depends on the dollar. From an objective point of view however, the United States has been broke for many years now, and every economist knows it.[i]

---

[i] Just how badly the US dollar is really doing can be seen in the fact that the American Federal Reserve has been calculating the current money supply on a monthly

What would happen if the dollar were suddenly worth nothing, if people actually stopped believing in it?

This would be the "worst case scenario" in this financial crisis because almost all global trade would collapse. The euro wouldn't help, nor would any other stable currency. The problem is that crude oil and many other commodities are traded in dollars. The dollar is the most commonly distributed currency in the world, and is recognized as a means of payment in almost every country.

If the United States were to go bankrupt and people were to lose confidence in the dollar, all dollar holders worldwide, not just Americans, would lose all of their assets from one day to the next, and global trade would collapse. This is why billions are flowing into banks and large enterprises as support. All of this money is meant to conceal the fact that we have long been overextending ourselves and that everything could collapse in an instant. These countries, these owners of central banks and money presses, want to use money to buy back our lost trust. And if we're lucky, it will work one more time.

If you now apply your healthy common sense and start to do your math like even just a mediocre businessman, the scales are bound to fall from your eyes: It can't go on like this forever. At some point our debts will catch up with us, the bubble will burst, and everyone will have to pay the piper.

Actually, after the real estate bubble in the United States burst, the next one was already in line: the credit bubble, and after that there will probably be a devaluation of American government securities through the rating agencies to deal with. Many economists are waiting for this bubble to collapse in the coming months. The effects will be more disastrous than we now dare to envision.

---

basis, but this figure stopped being made public in 2006.

The Challenge is Not the Crisis, but What Comes After – How Crises Create New Crises

Since I have been a central banker, I've learned
to mumble with great incoherence.
If I seem unduly clear to you,
you must have misunderstood what I said.[44]

Alan Greenspan
(former Chairman of the US Central Bank Federal Reserve System,
born 1926)

Let's suppose that the billions that are flowing into support programs for banks with bad credit (and that is every bank) are successful. Let's suppose that trust can be restored among banks and between citizens and their own banks. Politicians, bankers and economists will pat each other on the backs, pop a lot of champagne bottle and say: "We straightened that out again, didn't we?"

Slowly but surely, the clockwork of the world economy will start to tick again. There is just one problem that people like to ignore: the lubrication in the form of newly printed money that was pumped into the market. The difficulty lies in the fact that there was no lubricant in the past; it was just created. For this reason, this money is called *fiat money*. *Fiat lux* is Latin and comes from Genesis in the Bible. Translated it means "Let there be light." Fiat money describes "Let there be money:"

The printing presses are fired up, and there it is.[i] It has no true value; it does not bear any relation to the sum of all goods and services – but who cares as long as enough people believe in the intrinsic value of the

---

[i] Even though I use the word "printing," only the smallest proportion of circulating money is printed or minted as coins. Money printing is thus not to be taken literally, but symbolically. Most of the money put into circulation by central banks is created electronically. It is a number on a bank statement, a number that can be chosen by the central bank and that is created from nothing. These numbers in the billions have no connection to real goods, they are nothing more than ephemeral ghosts haunting the cathedrals of the capital.

money?

This is normally no problem, in the end every currency in the world is fiat money – money from nothing.

The acquisition of worldwide property, as described in the previous chapter, was likewise financed by fiat money. The World Authority for Currency and Land prints the money that it needs for the purchase of land. This is no problem for the money supply because the money has a connection to a real value through the land on the globe.

But even when the money supply *temporarily* exceeds the sum of all goods and services and the value of real estate, there are normally no difficulties as long as people are convinced of the value of the money. The emphasis here is on *temporarily*, because therein lies the problem. *Temporarily* only exists in theory. In practice there is no possibility to reduce the excess of money. It is like in Goethe's *Faust*: "*Sir, the need is great! The spirits that I summoned up, I now can't rid myself of.*"[45]

We can make money from nothing, but once created it stays in circulation and to date no one has come up with a realistic solution for taking that money back out of circulation. This is not exactly true however, because there are indeed solutions, for instance an incineration plant. This is often used for paper money in order to regulate the supply of cash. For virtual money, so-called deposit money which exists only in your account or in international payment flows, it doesn't work.

Firstly, no central bank can get money that it has put into circulation back into its possession; secondly, if this were possible, the bank would have to take it from its current owner. That, however, would be theft or expropriation, which is entirely unfair because it would affect only individuals.[i]

For now, we have to live with the excess money. I say "for now" because later I will propose a very simple solution for how the money could be cautiously removed from the economic cycle.

---

[i] The economically logical way to reduce the money supply would be for banks and nations to balance their debts with the central banks and with each other, and for the central banks to eliminate the repaid amounts. The global burden of debt is, however, much too high for this. No nation would risk this measure because it could lead to a deep recession. Another alternative is a currency reform, but this method is very risky and has potential for many injustices.

In the past, it was necessary to understand why too little money is a problem for your wallet even if it is no problem for the global economy, and why an excess of money always creates new crises.

So let's suppose that the current financial crisis is overcome. The markets have healed themselves, trust has been restored, and the back-patting has turned into strong confidence.

There is an enormous amount of money in circulation because trillions were flooded into the banks and the economy to prevent the crisis and many billions were already put there during the last crisis, the dotcom bubble in 2001.[46] But they were good investments because they seemed to have done the job: The markets are booming, employees are earning more than ever. Things are on the rise, and everyone wants to get in on it. Everyone wants not just a morsel, but a real piece of the pie. People with money are happy and people with more money want to invest it profitably in the promising future.

The problem is, however, that there not a sufficient supply of good financial investments to meet the demand for a high yield. A huge amount of money floods the market because its owners want to take part in the growth boom that, this time, will last forever.

No problem – why, after all, do we have bankers, investment bankers, financial engineers and all kinds of creative personnel who make their living from inventing new investment products with ever-higher interest rates?

An old saying goes: "Opportunity makes the thief." This is just such an opportunity, and only the truly reckless will make a real profit.

You are less interested in all that because you trust your money – provided that the boom took away the pressure of your debts – you trust your bank, your pension fund, or your life insurance. Everything should be legitimate and safe.

But only you believe that!

Where do you think the surpluses from your life insurance or your pension fund come from? Why does your bank pay you interest?

Because, of course, your money is *working*. Because it has long been fed back into the international financial cycle on the search for the next big win.

But, as I said earlier: The money supply has increased, and all that money wants to get out among the people. The investors now have to come up with something, for instance more vacation resorts with golf courses on the Spanish coast, artificial cities in the desert of California or, for a change, maybe Siberian gold mines.

And many people will be investing again because their money will be profitably applied. Money that's just lying around isn't working for you; it isn't creating new money from today to tomorrow. Also, this time it seems that the financial market is significantly more regulated, that people learned from the last crisis and have built safety nets; now everything is done right.

That may be true, but there is *one* thing that hasn't changed: There is significantly more money on the market than there was before the crisis and all that money is trying to multiply.

And because the volume of all money has in the meantime risen far above the sum of all available goods and services, it has no real foundation anymore. Just like last time, many people will get no more for their investments than hot air.

This new growth bubble will – like all of its predecessors and all of its successors – burst; and every time the effects will be more dramatic. With every crisis, more money has to be pumped into the market, and every time the gap will grow wider between the value of money and the goods and services backing it.

The fact that the last bubble will burst along with the rest is as certain as death and taxes.

Let's summarize a bit up to this point: The sum of all the world's money should, according to monetary theory, relate directly to the sum of all of the goods, services, and land available in the world. If this is true, then the money supply is balanced and is a consistent means of exchange for these various goods and services. Money has its value. Currently, that is not the case because some countries have printed significantly more money than can be related to actual value. This was done because there wasn't enough money at hand to finance large endeavors, like wars, for example. These countries are in debt. They have bought goods from other countries and paid with their printed money. Usually that works fine – but only as long as everyone is convinced of the value of this printed money and the economic power of these countries. The other countries hope that these countries will at some point be able to pay their debts.

In the United States, that point is far off because that country will probably never be able to pay its dollar debts. But that doesn't matter as long as almost all countries trade their commodities in dollars and continue to trust the dollar. However, if this belief dissolves, then the world will be bankrupt. Because no one wants that – neither the Germans, the Russians, nor the Chinese – the United States can go on printing money.

Now shake your head and ask yourself why other countries do this too.

It's simple: One of the most important commodities for any economy is crude oil. Without gas, no cars could drive, no ships could sail, and no airplanes could fly. Without oil there would be no plastic, and without oil many places would lose their energy supply. And if the oil tank in your cellar is empty, you'll have no heat.

But what does oil have to do with the dollar?

Without the dollar, you can't buy crude oil. No crude oil-exporting country will sell you its oil for euros, yen, or anything else. An agreement between OPEC[47] (Organization of Petroleum Exporting Countries) and the United States dictates that crude oil can only be traded in dollars.[48] There was another country that wanted to trade oil in other currencies: Iraq under the leadership of Saddam Hussein.[49] You see what happened: The country is in ruins. Only the crude oil industry is being revived – of course under the direction of American petroleum corporations.

But back to money. Every time more money is printed, the money supply increases. And when the money supply increases, it is backed all the less by the sum of all available goods, services, and land in the world. There is, therefore, more money in the world than would be necessary for countertrade.

In an economic crisis, this money stays in vaults and accounts because everyone who has money holds onto it. Markets are fearful. As soon as a crisis is overcome, this mass of money will flood into the market and try to multiply itself. People want to take part in the upcoming boom.

Now there is significantly more money on the market than there are solid and material countervalues. For this reason, many investments will be fantasies, bubbles without any connection to reality. These bubbles will burst again; more money will be printed to absorb the next crisis. But when more money is printed, the money supply increases – and so on until the bitter end: the final crisis.

Many people will object at this point: But in a crisis money disappears, entire fortunes are destroyed.

That's not true! No dollar, euro, yen, or yuan is lost in a crisis. The money just changes hands – where there are losers, there are also winners. Money doesn't get lost. Once a money supply has been created, it cannot be reduced by conventional economic means.

I would like to clarify in two examples why money does not disappear, even in a major crisis.

The current financial crisis started when the speculative bubble in the American real estate market burst. In order to buy a nice house, people borrowed money from their banks. Banks allowed them generous credit because, in the case that the owners couldn't pay their debts, the house itself and the land were mortgaged to the bank. The house was financed by a bank and this money flowed into the accounts of real estate and construction companies, etc. That's where most of it still is. If the home owners can't pay their debts to their banks, their mortgages, the house goes back to the bank and is foreclosed. The proceeds of a foreclosure are, however, often less than the amount the bank used to finance the house. So the bank loses money. As a taxpayer, you are supposed to compensate for this loss exactly. The bank hopes that you will be held responsible for the fact that there was no proper assessment carried out during the financing process. The so-called junk bonds [i] that everyone is talking about are nothing more than the debts of former homeowners that the banks traded amongst themselves, because everyone wanted a piece of the big pie. If the banks receive

---

[i] The trading of the financial instruments called junk bonds are part of so-called 'credit default swaps' (CDS): A CDS is a form of credit insurance. In real estate, a CDS is derived from a mortgage backed security. These were invented in the nineties by the New York investment banker Lewis Ranieri, and were used for many years in the coverage of mortgage loans. Their function is simple: A bank bundles several different credit contracts. In a credit bundle, there are always many good and some bad credit contracts hiding; usually the majority are good ones. In the next step, the bank borrows money from another bank and offers its bundle as collateral. The bank that sells the CDS thus disperses its risk and gets new money. The bank that buys the CDS makes a profit through fees, interest, and risk charges. As long as there are only a few credit defaults, everybody makes a profit. If, however, many homebuyers can't pay their debts, the whole system suddenly collapses and every bank that has bought a CDS is thrown into the maelstrom. A crisis like this doesn't happen because some greedy bankers packed too many bad credit contracts into a bundle, but because almost none of the credit contracts were properly evaluated and too many people believed in never-ending growth.

grants for their "bad credit," the money supply would have to increase, because the money that the bank lent to the homebuyers didn't just get lost. In the meantime, the value of the house has simply fallen.

This is exactly how it was in 2001 during the internet stock bubble: Money from investors flowed into companies without substance. In this case, too, many agents, banks, etc. made money. It's also true that one or two years later the stocks fell to just a few cents, or to zero. All the same, real money was flowing at the beginning, and many people made a fine living from it – many are still doing so. But in this case too, no money went missing; the value of the stocks just fell.

As you can see, money can be made from nothing. But it doesn't just disappear. For money, the following rule always applies: What one person loses, another person wins. In the current crisis, many people are losing, but there are winners too: The holders of so-called speculative funds.

In order to really understand this, we have to go deeper into the nature of money and the fundamentals of speculation – and explore the question of why the poor get poorer and the rich get richer.

Money –
The Only Product without an Expiration Date

The most hated sort, and with the greatest reason, is usury,
which makes a gain out of money itself, and not from the natural
object of it.
For money was intended to be used in exchange, but not to increase
at interest. And this term interest, which means the birth of money
from money, is applied to the breeding of money because the off-
spring resembles the parent.[50]

Aristotle
(Greek philosopher, 384 – 322 BCE.)

Up to this point I have, if in a very simplified manner, presented the causes and the course of the last financial crisis. It has become clear that there is no direct escape from this spiral – unless we reduced the money supply and changed the nature of money to remove part of its speculative character.

Why is it even possible to speculate with money?

Why does money accrue interest? How are goods different from money?

Apples, pears, milk, and even cars have an expiration date. Food goes bad and becomes unsalable. Cars don't mold, but technology advances, and who wants to buy an outdated model? Even natural resources have no constant value because no one knows for sure if there are still undiscovered sources somewhere that will create a sudden oversupply and lead to lower prices.

Commodities have to be sold while they are fresh and can get an adequate price. This applies to labor and services too because a service that is performed today can't be retrieved tomorrow. Your life moves inexorably towards its end; your time is limited. For this reason, a service that can't be sold today is lost tomorrow. Also, when you aren't able to sell your services, in times of unemployment, you may be slowly but surely losing knowledge, ability, and motivation.

Whether you deal in apples or your own muscles as a day laborer, you have to bring your goods or your own skin to the market to find a buyer. You may need to lower your price because you are competing with many other apple sellers or day laborers. But maybe apples are in short supply and you get more money for your goods than you expected. But you should never forget that your freshly picked apples won't look so nice by tomorrow. You may need to make a compromise and meet your buyer with a price halfway. If you don't, your apples may rot and may soon not even be usable for apple sauce. After all, the old saying goes: "A bird in the hand is better than two in the bush."

Pricing is not just based on supply and demand, as you probably learned in school; instead every seller is constantly under pressure to dispose of his or her goods. According to how perishable it is and how much money the seller needs, the price for a commodity can fluctuate substantially. Sellers are always subject to the pressure of time because their goods are perishable.

If you are successful, what you get in exchange for what you brought to the market is money. Money is a means of exchange, and if you are an apple seller you can buy, for instance, pears with the money you earn, or pay a day laborer to help you with the harvest. You can also put the money aside and hoard it because as soon as you've sold your apples, nothing bad can happen. Money doesn't mold. You have guided your perishable harvest safely into the harbor of money.

The example of apples applies to every other commodity, service, and even to labor.

By transforming your commodity into money, you have made an ephemeral, perishable product into a certainty. The holder of a commodity has become the holder of money, a capitalist.

The holders of commodities have to sell their goods or else they will lose value. Money, however, does not share this characteristic. This is why capitalists have power. They exploit it shamelessly – so do we all.

It's why we keep going to the market. The apple seller who has money in his pocket now wants to buy pears. Instead of going straight to his neighbor and buying them, he waits across from the stand and watches the business for a while.

From his own experience, the apple seller knows that the goods will be cheaper in the evening than they were in the morning. He knows that all of the pears the pear seller doesn't sell today will have a bargain price just one day later. They may be a little blotchy, and people will haggle for them. The price can only go down.

The apple seller is speculating with the money in his pocket on when he can buy the pears for the cheapest price. He can do it too, because unlike the pears at the stand, the cash in his wallet has no expiration date.

You see: Speculating is already possible without even mentioning the word interest. Speculation is in the nature of money: It is because money has no expiration date.[i]

The British economist John Maynard Keynes wrote, in summary: The fact that money, if one possesses it, has practically no disadvantages makes it risk-free for money holders to hold their money back from an offer and hoard it if their buying power doesn't seem high enough, or if they expect it to increase. Thus, with speculative intentions, money is taken out of the economic cycle and kept in speculative funds. It disappears into the so-called liquidity trap.[51]

"Liquidity trap" means simply that there is enough money, but not enough of it available on the market. It's hiding in a savings box. This savings box contains all the money that seems to disappear without a trace from the international cash flow during a financial crisis. It is not, however, gone, lost, or burned, as you may believe. If some people lose money in speculation, other people have gained it. The money just changes hands. And the new money holder puts it aside during a crisis: He or she divests it for a time from the economic cycle.

Money and currency speculators do nothing different from the apple seller: They hang onto their money. Because banks and investment funds work with money in huge dimensions, this leads to a shortage, a lack of money available on the market.

Weren't we just talking about a much too large money supply – and now it's suddenly too small?

Both are the case: The worldwide money supply is much too large because too much money has been printed. And when all of this money flows into the market, in the next five to ten years it is sure to cause another financial crisis. At the moment, however, nothing is flowing because the

---

[i] This kind of speculation is called a "put." With a put, one can do excellent business in times of downturn, because it speculates on falling prices.

money is hiding in the savings boxes of banks, investment funds, and speculators. It is missing from the market. This is why many countries' stimulus programs are pumping money into the market. It is a strenuous attempt to move banks and speculators to break their piggy banks. What's curious about it is that the same people who are holding onto their own money receive part of your tax money as an incentive to open their savings boxes.[i]

"That's insanity," you'll say, and ask: Why go through all that?

The reason is as follows: The nature of money that makes hoarding and speculation possible can lead to the most dangerous form of economic crises – deflation. Deflation describes a situation where, put simply, the rule of supply and demand stops working because, despite falling prices, no one wants to buy anything anymore. Everyone hopes that what's cheap today will be cheaper tomorrow. This retention of money from the market is, however, only possible because money has no expiration date and cannot go bad. Our apple seller salutes this fact.

As a result of deflation almost everything becomes cheaper, and no one wants to pay the real vale for anything anymore. Perhaps some readers are celebrating now and shouting: "Cheap? Finally – this is what I've been waiting for!" But don't celebrate too early, because during deflation not only the prices of goods fall – salaries fall too. And if they don't fall, they certainly don't rise. No one profits from deflation, not even bargain hunters. Deflation has the strongest effect on the poorest in the value chain, particularly those who deliver commodities or produce them at starvation wages.

And what happens to all of the withheld money?

---

[i] Of course banks don't report on their balance sheets the money that they hold back from the market. Then everyone would see, and there would be no subsidies. It is somewhat more tricky: In order to gamble above the level allowed by bank supervision, banks found so-called special purpose vehicles. Often, these are in tax havens, but they are always founded in countries with strict bank confidentiality. In good times, banks speculate with these special purpose vehicles, and in bad times they park their money in them. Money that is never meant to show up on their balance sheets. Only the bank has access to its special purpose vehicle, no one else: No nation, tax auditor, or law enforcement body has access to them. In boom times, regulatory authorities have allowed this actually illegal practice, but now it is coming home to roost. This doesn't mean that every bank that is profiting from state subsidies has some money hidden away in a special purpose vehicle. Most, however, almost certainly do.

It stays for some while in the speculation funds, in the savings boxes. As soon as the economy starts to recover, however, this money and the money that central banks create in every crisis (in the currency-increasing plans described in the last section) floods the market in ever more complex and intransparent financial products that promise ever higher profits for even small savers.

Why Money Has to Flow

A slow progress holds some promise,
but to stand still promises failure.[52]

Chinese proverb

Now you know the whole truth: Your money is hiding along with far too many billions in dubious speculation funds and the entire world economy is in a liquidity trap. Money isn't flowing anymore, and the global economic motor is stalling. Sometimes it stutters a little more, but that will stop too and despite all of the new billions, a dead silence falls over the land.

The river has dried up and the time has come again when the chances of making it flow again are next to nothing.

There is a saying attributed to Karl Marx that goes: "The earth will be either vibrantly red or it will be blood red" . By "vibrantly red," Marx meant the red of the communist banner. Indeed, this banner is not being hoisted. Instead, the naked battle for survival will begin because if the river runs dry, all of the money in the world will be worth nothing.

In that case, capitalism will be as much as a failure as the attempts of communism and socialism. Trust in nations and central banks, and the belief in the value of money will have entirely dissolved. And don't start to think that this will be a slow process! Once the situation gets to a certain point, it happens – even if politicians tell you differently – maybe not overnight, but within a few days.

What exactly happens can be described in a few phrases: Because money has no value anymore, an all-encompassing fight breaks out for staple foods, heating oil, and gas – at least as long as there are reserves. You can't buy anything anymore because no one wants your worthless money. And while the last hidden stockpiles are still being plundered, a black market is slowly established: Eggs for rice, medicine for prostitution, gas for contract murder. There won't be any fresh supplies because there will be no money to buy goods. The situation will then probably develop into one that we have only seen on television – uprisings and riots. Right here, in the middle of America and Europe, in the middle of our civilized and developed world. As opposed to developing countries we have the great disadvantage that we have not learned to deal with such situations. We are less used to improvisation and hang on the thread of high technology that could become worthless overnight. In any case, you can't eat it.

Everyone who deals with this issue is afraid of this day – very afraid.

But it doesn't need to go that far if we act quickly and change our course. It is indeed late, but not too late.

How can we turn the dried-up ditch into a roaring river and at the same time reduce the money supply in speculative funds? How is it possible to persuade banks, investment funds, and speculators to break their piggy banks?

First of all: it is possible.

We must once again, as for the distribution of the world's land, open our minds to unfamiliar thoughts. We have to find a way to slowly reduce the money supply to a normal level – a way that favors not money holders, but commodity holders, tradesmen, producers, that is everyone who is involved in the processes that produce real goods.

Let's go back once more to the apple seller with the money in his pocket who is speculating on whether pears will be cheaper in the evening or on the next day. He can only do that because cash doesn't lose value. If his money were worth less in the course of an afternoon, he would be forced into action, at least if he really wanted pears.

This is the same way that banks, rich people, and speculators behave. They withdraw their money from the economic cycle because stockpiling and hoarding doesn't cost anything and their money doesn't lose value. They wait, like the apple seller, for better times.

Now let's suppose that this was impossible because money that's not spent loses its value from day to day. Under this assumption, the money in savings boxes would be worth a little less every day. This loss can be minimal; it's enough if just a little bit is shaved off. It doesn't have to hurt, the money holder just has to feel it.

Banks and speculators would then have every reason to get their money out among the people as quickly as possible.

The money would flow out of savings boxes and into the market – without any state incentives. If it didn't it would be worth less tomorrow than today.[i].

No one likes to lose. There would be no more reason for either small savers or speculators to hold onto money and wait for a bargain to come knocking and for goods to be cheaper. Money would have to be spent because if it were just lying around, it would lose value.

The result of this kind of money with automatic depreciation would be such that state stimulus programs would be unnecessary for starting up the economic motor and getting people to start buying more and to even start storing goods. For instance, you would refill your heating oil tank even at the beginning of the summer because your heating oil wouldn't go bad, but your money would.

Could it go on that way forever?

Definitely not, and the buying frenzy would at some point even out to a normal level. The roaring river would become a normal flow, at the latest when the money made from nothing by central banks in recent years started to lose more and more value.

The flow would start to calm down when a balance was reached be-

---

[i] This kind of money is also called "Freigeld." Examples of such a money system exist in Egypt ("grain currency") in the first century BCE and in the Middle Ages in Europe.

In Ptolemaic Egypt, grain was used as money; it was loaded into granaries and ceramic pieces were distributed as a proof of ownership. These pieces were then used as money in economic life. Once could collect this grain minus a certain deduction taken each year for spoiled grain and storage costs. This system emerged between 322 and 330 BCE; after the conquest of Egypt by the Romans, the Roman system of coin money was introduced.

In the Middle Ages in Europe, coin money (e.g. bracteates) was declared invalid by local lords and clergy in certain situations and was exchanged for new coins minus a deduction for the minting. The intervals varied from several times annually to once every 7 years, and the deductions ranged from 15% to 40%. The difference went to the lords or the clergy. This was practiced principally between the years 1075 and 1400. Due to problems with managing the increased money supply, silver melting losses in minting, and pressure from business people who wanted lasting, far-reaching money, this so-called "coin discrediting" was abandoned and replaced with trading and purchasing taxes.

During this time, both economic areas achieved major cultural feats (almost all cathedrals were built during this time) and material prosperity among their populations; after changing their monetary systems, both areas began to decline.

tween the supply of available money and the sum of all goods and services.

Until this time comes, and it will take two to four generations, every money holder will spend his or her money. And that's the trick: The money that can't be spent will disappear. It will slowly disappear from the market, and indeed forever.

We will rid ourselves of the spirits we called up. Until then we can celebrate the party, and it will be a real party – not with speculative money, but with real, genuine goods.

John Maynard Keyes called this form of depreciation "gentle inflation" and added that one additional percent of inflation is preferable to one additional percent of unemployment.[53] The word inflation here does not stand for the specter of hyperinflation as in the years 1932 and later. It means a measured devaluation of the money in speculation funds that is being withheld from the market.

Concretely, it works like this: Usually you get interest and compound interest for the balance in your account. Gentle inflation works just the same way, but in reverse: Each month, a minimal portion of hoarded or even saved money is removed.

Now I hear: "Then something will be taken from me after all."

Just wait! In the next section I will explain why, even though a minimal amount is deducted from the money in your bank, you wouldn't suffer any losses, but would end up with more money in your wallet.

So suspend your disbelief and ask yourself why politicians and economists don't use this strategy. There are two answers.

The first is, this method is only possible on a global level: only if all nations act together. Otherwise the money will just flee into another currency or into another country, to a place in the sun where it doesn't lose value. Money is extremely clever and will find every hidden loophole. Moreover: Do you believe that politicians would agree as long as they are all hoping to find a speculative bargain between their country and some other country?

Definitely not.

You should know: It's not just individual speculators and fund managers that make a profit from the current nature of money – it's nations. For example, exporting countries like Germany and China have made a significant profit from the current bubble. In contrast, countries that already had nothing have lost even more. It is as it always has been: The poor are getting poorer and the rich are getting richer.

At this point I will summarize once more: The economic motor is stalling all over the world because banks, investors, and speculators don't trust each other or the market anymore. For this reason, the largest supplies of money are hiding in enormous, safeguarded savings boxes, and are missing from the market. Hardly any company or private person can get credit anymore, and so investments are running dry. There are fewer new cars, machinery, and other goods sold every day. There is a danger that manufacturers will start to lower the prices of their goods to be able to make any sales at all. If prices are lower, wages have to be lower too. And the less people earn, the less they can buy. This spiral is called deflation and is the most dangerous of all economic crises because it can lead to the collapse of the entire monetary system. If this happens, all of the world's money will be worth nothing within a few days. The result would be struggles for resources, riots, and the collapse of our developed world. That's why every country pumps billions into its banks and industries in an economic crisis: They want to avoid collapse.

But there is another way to prevent the economic motor from stalling that doesn't require state incentives. If money were to automatically lose value from day to day, there would no longer be a reason to keep it in a savings box. It would flood into the market because otherwise it would lose its buying power. This has the side effect of leveling the money supply over a long period of time so that it is equal to the sum of all available goods, services, and land. The surplus money would disappear through a gentle, but rising automatic depreciation.

Don't confuse this depreciation with a tax on saved money. A tax would just change the ownership of part of the money, for instance from the hands of speculators into those of the state. But that doesn't reduce the money supply, the cause of all financial crises.

This brings us to the second answer to the question of why the concept of gentle inflation has not yet been put into practice. It affects all people equally.

Why You'll Have More Money in Your Pocket even though Your Saved Money doesn't Yield Interest

A chap who speculates - let this be said -. is very like a beast on moorland dry,
That by some evil spirit round and round is led,
While fair, green pastures round about him lie.[54]

Johann Wolfgang von Goethe
(German author, 1749–1832)

You would like to provide for the future so that you'll have a pleasant old age, or maybe you would just like to put some money aside. You would like to save up for future investments. So you look for a safe investment, a parking spot for your money, so to speak. But look out: With a parking spot you pay a fee to leave your car there, if that spot isn't in a supermarket. But you want more from an investment, whether this investment is life insurance or a savings account. You want interest. You want to get money for parking it.

What world do you live in? What garage has ever paid out money? Something seems illogical.

You may argue that a bank can *work* with the money that you deposit, and that you want a part of the profit.

How in heaven's name is the bank supposed to work with your money? Does the parking spot work with your car? Do other people drive it while you go shopping? I would like to see your face if someone did that!

You expect things from your money that you can't imagine for other things, like your car. You expect your money to work for you; and that while you're sleeping, it should make you, if not rich, at least wealthier. And with traditional money, money without an integrated expiration date, that is possible: You give it to your bank, your bank gives it to someone else and they pay a kind of usage fee called interest. The bank, in turn, gives part of that interest back to you. That's how everyone makes money – at least that's what people tell you.

With the new, slowly self-depreciating money, that doesn't work anymore. You can be glad if find a bank that takes it and maybe reduces or prevents creeping losses. But you can forget about interest. The new money doesn't have speculation fees, and interest is nothing other than that.

Money has become a commodity, like a car. If you want to park it, you have to pay.

I can hear you saying: You don't want this new money anymore, this money with an expiration date. It would be too good to have a world without speculators or economic crises, with only advantages for you. But now this drawback, when interest for fixed deposits is up to seven percent at many banks; and money in your personal speculation fund, your fixed deposit account, can really work for you.

It's true: With the new money, you don't get any more risk-free interest as a mini-speculator and small saver. But you won't lose anything either; instead you'll make a profit that far exceeds the former interest. And you'll see this profit in your wallet or in your account. Your balance will increase, even though you won't be getting any interest.

Now you are excited to know how that might work, because now this money with an expiration date might make sense after all.

The explanation is simple: If there is no interest, you spend less money because the goods and services that you buy will be cheaper, and will contribute more than interest to your savings balance.

Once more from the beginning: You bring your hard-earned money to the bank and put it into a savings account. The bank, in turn, has many customers that need money – for instance, the baker next door who wants to buy a new bread baking machine. And since the baker has a lot of loyal customers like you, he gets credit. That means that the bank loans the baker the money to buy the latest bread baking machine. The baker, of course, has to pay that money back in the coming years, and with a surcharge. The bank doesn't give the baker the money for free; it gets interest. The investment makes sense for the baker anyway, and the new machine is paid off in three years. That is daily business.

But where does the baker get the money for the interest that he owes the bank?

It's simple: he, like every businessman, calculates a so-called *capital cost* and a *financing cost* into the price of his bread. This inevitably makes the bread more expensive. This is true of all investments that manufactures and merchants make: They are calculated into the price of products, and in the end you as the buyer and consumer pay a price that includes the interest entrepreneurs pay to their banks.

Are you still wondering why things always get more expensive?

This continuous price increase is caused by the interest that banks take for lending money. If you compare the rate of price increases in the last year with the interest that your bank paid you for your savings account, you'll see what a terrible hit you've been taking. The banks are pocketing the biggest piece of the pie, and they use it to build dazzling glass towers. You, as a small saver, bleed to death: from low interest for your saved money and rising fees for things like your account management and your credit card. Even the interest for the money lent to build the bank's skyscrapers is put back onto you.

You may argue that many banks offer free account management. That's true – but only to get your money and to lend it for a fee. Even these alleged gifts come back around to you at some point in the form of prices that are higher than they have to be. The second reason why "money with an expiration date" isn't in circulation and why we stumble from one crisis to the next is, as shown, the problem of interest – and it affects everyone who profits from interest, yourself included.

If all products are cheaper, and by a significantly higher percentage than the interest you get from your bank – if such a money reform would leave you with more money in your wallet, then there's no reason to regret the loss of interest.

The requirement is, however, that the interest a bank gets for extending credit falls to zero. Borrowers, whether they be corporations or individuals, would then have no capital and financing costs, and nearly every product could be cheaper.

In order to get this so-called money market interest rate to zero, we have to consider automatic depreciation rates for hoarded money. Too low is no good because then money would not flow into the market. Too high is dangerous, because then there is a danger of run-away inflation. Most probably it would be enough right now if the rate were somewhere between two and five percent. With every new crisis and an increasing money supply, the depreciation rate will have to rise because more money is always seeping into the market, and it will have to be removed.

Some people will now begin to talk about the self-depreciating money as expropriation. That's not the case, because where does the money come from in the first place?

It is the central bank's money, which is created in every crisis to absorb the excrescence of speculative bubbles. It is money without value, which hurts the global community. Moreover, every money holder is free to invest in real commodities such as buildings or company shares to avoid the devaluation of his or her own money. There can, therefore be no question of expropriation; it is a question of a measure to be taken in financial and global politics that is no different than changing the prime rate.[i] The only difference is that this interest is currently seen as negative.

---

[i] The prime rate means the interest rate at which commercial banks can borrow money from the central bank.

How the New Money Prevents Speculation and Economic Crises

There is nothing so dangerous as the pursuit
of a rational investment policy in an irrational world.[55]

John Maynard Keynes

Now you know the whole drama and understand why, despite all political assurances, no one is really interested in making the economic system fair and just for everyone. As long as there is someone like you out there paying the piper, everything is just fine for the people who make money from money.

An old saying goes: "The last one out has to carry the pay." The fatal fact of economics is that the last one is always the poorest one – the one who has no capital and has only his or her skin to bring to the market. And that affects not only the poorest of the poor in the developing countries, who I discussed in the last chapter, but an increasing number of people in the industrial nations as well. You can read about it in every newspaper: In recent years, the gap between rich and poor has been growing fatally wide in almost every country, and what was previously a solid middle class is now an endangered species in many places. With every new crisis, the gap between rich and poor will continue to increase. Wealth will be divided among an increasingly smaller group of people, while an increasingly larger group of people, those who are paying the piper, will be trying to make ends meet.

But supposing that self-depreciating money were to be introduced on a worldwide scale – what would be the result?

First of all, a huge amount of money would flow into the market; banks and speculators in particular would buy up the entire market for precious metals and stones. The prices for such nonperishable goods would shoot up to unimaginable heights. As I have explained, money tends towards any haven that seems at least halfway safe. Furthermore, every available repository would be filled with edible goods, oil, gas, etc. – any goods that could be stored. Money that has become itself a good through gradual devaluation would try to hide behind storable products.

But stop! That won't work at all, because what could diamond and gold dealers get with their money? They have goods, and they would be stupid to exchange them for money that would just lose value.

So very little would actually happen. Markets would not explode and prices would not rise to immeasurable levels. There would be no new global need for cold storage. Hardly anyone with goods that are imperishable and have a stable value would want the new money. So there would be no shortage of commodities or food.

The majority of the money will stay where it is: in vaults and in accounts in Liechtenstein, the Cayman Islands, or the Bahamas.

The money that makes the economic motor run will flow pretty quickly, and without interest, because there is after all enough of it. And all of the excess money will slowly but surely lose its value, simply because no one needs it.

All of this leads to neither rising prices, that is to say inflation, nor to falling prices because nothing more will happen than the market equalizing itself to the necessary volume of money. In this process every asset without a countervalue, every speculative asset, will disappear.

That does not, however, mean that the rich will get poorer. No luxury yacht, no bottle of champagne, and no bars of gold will disappear – but money that doesn't flow will evaporate by and by. Money will be a commodity like any other.

Is there a catch?

There aren't any known ones; in any case I couldn't find any in the literature on the issue.

But how will it be possible to earn money at all?

That's a good question, but it too has a simple answer: by creating value and by producing goods. By doing all of the things that were lost during the era of investment banking and fast money: producing and refining material goods.

And of course you can still speculate with the new money to a certain degree by betting and gambling – why should that be forbidden? But gambling will no longer force into poverty those who have nothing to do with it.

In order to explain that, I will provide a short and very simplified description of what defines speculation, and how it is different from normal business.

When you buy something for little and sell it for more, that's business: You have transport costs, storage costs, and much more; and so you have a right to get a risk fee and an entrepreneurial profit. You are a business person, like those that have existed since biblical times.

Speculation, however, is something very different. Speculators don't deal with goods or with risk; instead they gamble on supply and demand in the world. There is an insider saying that goes: "Where blood lines the streets is where the most money will be made."[56]

But slow down: The requirement for speculation is always a lack or an imminent lack of vital commodities, for example crude oil, food, or a lack of medicine during a deadly epidemic.

An example: A speculative fund buys all of the stores of heating oil in a certain country for a very good price. In the contracts with the mineral oil companies, it is stipulated that the speculation fund, which has no tank farms or anything of the like, pays for the oil at the end of the year and either keeps it or sells it back to the mineral oil companies. Until then, it stays where it is: in the tank. Something like this is only possible with a large amount of money, but speculation funds have more money that you would believe. This type of speculation is called commodities futures.

Now it's autumn and many homeowners want to fill up the heating oil tanks behind their houses. But there is no heating oil – it has already been sold. There is now a scarcity of heating oil. Not really – the tanks are actually full, but there is a large demand on the market. The longer the scarcity lasts, the higher the price for oil rises. The speculative fund then waits a while before selling the heating oil back to the mineral oil companies, and everyone has made a good profit. Everyone except the consumers who pay the piper in the form of an artificially raised price.

Speculative business like this happens every day all around the globe. Sometimes they are disguised as oil or food shortages, but they are always connected to important commodities.[i] For example, shortly before the beginning of the current financial crisis, in mid-2008, speculators worldwide had driven up the prices of crude oil, wheat, and rice, and many countries were thrown into bloody uprisings. Bertold Brecht wrote about this seventy years ago in one of his plays: "Famines don't break out, they are made."[57]

---

[i] This kind of speculation is called a "call." It is a bet on rising prices, which are themselves often caused by speculation itself.

This abhorrent kind of speculation will, not entirely but partially, disappear when the new money is introduced.

There are two reasons for this: First, merchants will only trade their goods for money after close consideration because if something goes wrong in terms of speculation, the money can lose value more quickly than the goods. But speculators will have lots of ideas; they will hold out the prospect of high profits and appeal to the merchants' greed.

The second point is more subtle but also more effective because it applies to the consumers: If money in the savings box slowly loses value, then it's not necessary to wait till the last minute to buy something – to wait until the other guy can be shaken down. It might be worth it even to keep reserves.

If you think back, the times when factories kept things in stock weren't too long ago. The disappearance of these stocks and the mode of delivering everything just in time have to do with the fact that money doesn't automatically lose value. No one would want their money to be stored away. If intermediate and long-term storage facilities were set up, all the air would be taken out of speculation because entrepreneurs with stocks of inventory wouldn't have to react right away to fluctuations in commodity prices. But the requirement for a return to stock keeping is, of course, that it add up.

With money that gradually loses value, that would be true in most cases. It wouldn't make speculation disappear completely, but it would put a curb on it: Speculators would hardly be able to cause catastrophes anymore.

But how will it be possible to make money? How can you still do some real gambling?

There is enough of that, so much will stay as it is. You can gamble on stocks and shares. You can still buy complicated financial instruments or keep dealing in commodities.

The only difference would be: You could cause less misery than you can today. Even if you speculate poorly, if a bubble bursts, the rest of humanity doesn't have to be afraid that the worldwide flow of capital will stall and run dry.

At the same time this new money will blow a cold wind in many people's faces because many people will see expropriation and will cry out: socialism, communism, dilettantism!

It is not a matter of expropriation, though, but one of money regaining its nature as a means of exchange for goods and services and losing a small part of its speculative character.

Once more: Interest for money that is borrowed by entrepreneurs is without exception paid for by consumers through higher prices. If the bank gets less interest, prices will gradually fall – in any case they won't rise.

For this reason, even though you don't get interest for your savings account and your saved money slowly loses value, you will have more money in your wallet or in your account than before, simply because prices will be lower. This doesn't just apply to individuals, but to companies because all products will have lower prices. No manufacturing company loses money from self-depreciating money – everyone profits. Even speculators and money holders who are investing in production facilities or new technologies will be rewarded because their money will stop degenerating as soon as they start financing real goods.

Only people who want to make money with money, people who hoard large sums of money, will lose part of their assets over two or three generations; but even so, there is still enough time to turn themselves from investment bankers into entrepreneurs.

The Missing Gear in the Machinery of Financial Management

Inflation is like nicotine or alcohol.
In small amounts, it's stimulating
just as long as you don't become a chain smoker or an alcoholic.[58]

André Kostolany
(stock and financial expert, speculator, 1906–1999)

At the beginning of this book, I compared the world economy to complex clockwork with a design flaw. The problematic gear in this machinery is called: perpetual growth. There is no such thing because the only thing that grows is the money supply. It's easy to see: Land, resources, and nature are limited. Where is there room for growth? When we talk about growth, we can only be talking about the money supply because everything else is limited and is out of our control.

There are, as previously described, two major economic cycles: boom and bust.

In a boom, everyone believes in a supposedly unlimited growth and invests their money in every kind of stock and business. Everybody wants to make a big profit at small expense. It's only human.

Because there is no such thing as perpetual growth, the long upward curve starts at some point to descend. A bust cycle begins – what is called an economic depression. At such a time, it is advisable to put the profits made during a boom cycle into a safe place. Thus, money disappears, as previously described, into those enormous piggy banks, the speculation funds. Economic circulation starts to stall, and in order to start it up again, states pump fresh money into it through their central banks.

For the most part, the motor does start again, the recession ends, and a new upswing begins – however, with more money in circulation.

To clarify: Take a plastic bucket and dump in pitcher after pitcher of new water. At some point the bucket will overflow.

That bucket is the financial market. The water in the bucket is the increasing money supply, and every pitcher that you pour in is another subsidy, another bank bailout, or another state stimulus program. There may be situations where putting state-printed money into circulation makes sense to avoid larger damages, for example right before a deflation when prices are sinking lower and lower, or when the money flow is threatening to stop altogether.

Nevertheless: What flows in has to flow back out, or else the bucket will spill over. Or you will have to dump everything out.

In the clockwork of our financial system, there is a gear that is responsible for getting money into the market but there is no gear for removing an excess of money. It would be a simple repair job to install another gear to correct this problem. But what is really needed is a check screw that can regulate when the clock should run faster or slower. A dial that can adjust the clock to the economic cycles. This dial would regulate the money supply by taking money out during an upswing and putting it in during a downturn.

At the moment, and for the next generations, that dial, however, has to be set to take money out – set to gentle inflation. For as long as it takes for the money supply on the market and in speculation funds to regain a justifiable relationship to the sum of all goods and services.

The problem of the missing gear, "gradual gentle inflation" lies in the fact that it can only function globally – only if it applies equally to all major currencies, or to a single world currency. If we don't install this part, the bucket will at some point overflow and in the worst case, be dumped out all at once.

That happened last in 1932, in the Great Depression, a worldwide economic crisis. There was no adjusting dial then for gentle inflation, and the result was that all of the world's money was devalued over the course of several months, which had dramatic effects all over the globe. It led to hyperinflation with extremely high unemployment and poverty, at the end of which was the Second World War.

It doesn't need to go that far this time.

5   Thinking and Acting Globally

A person has three ways to learn wisdom:
the first is contemplation, that is the most noble,
the second is imitation, that is the easiest,
and the third is experience, that is the bitterest.[59]

Confucius (Chinese philosopher, 551 – 479 BCE)

Vision and Humanity

It is not the function of the poet
to relate what has happened,
but what may have happened —
what is possible according to the law of probability or necessity.[60]

Aristotle
(Greek philosopher, 384 – 322 BCE.)

Have I promised you too much with my vision of a fair economic order? Has anything been taken away from anyone?

No.

The property reform leaves only winners: Current land owners get more capital in their pockets; the unpropertied get a global unconditional basic income and a large degree of additional buying power. Everyone profits.

The monetary reform creates a situation where your money doesn't yield interest, but on the other hand, the rate of price increase falls and goods become cheaper. This gives you more money in your pockets in the end. In addition, you get the global unconditional basic income.

These reforms may add up for you because no one will stop you from engaging in speculative business and earning money. Nothing is limited or restricted by the state. You can go on as you always have. You will just no longer be in the position to cause great harm. The gradual depreciation of the new money also causes no expropriation or confiscation because those who invest in real goods will be rewarded. Everyone can win without there being a loser.

You shake your head contemplatively and point to all of the difficulties of implementing this plan.

You're right: The difficulties of implementation will be enormous, but as long as you argue against it, you are missing the gravity of the situation. The world and the financial system are standing at the edge of an abyss. Or do you think that countries are issuing billions in stimulus programs just for fun?

The physicist and rocket scientist Wernher von Braun once said:

"Everything that humanity can imagine is possible."[61] First, however, we have to have the bitterest experiences to move us. Until a global change in the economic and financial system comes, until fairness and justice rule on this planet, many more people will die of hunger and preventable illnesses. From every single one of these people, other people have made a profit.

Until now, we have only known these catastrophes to happen in the third world. With every global speculative bubble that bursts, with every economic crisis, however, the threat comes closer to us. In the United States alone, the number of people living on the margins of subsistence has rapidly increased in recent years and even in socially well-insured Europe, soup kitchens and child poverty are everyday occurrences.

All of this is effect of a few small gears in the economic machinery that aren't working right. For a while during the good years, the boom years, we liked to overlook this fact because we were profiting from these mistakes and the specter of poverty wasn't looming over us.

Those times are over.

Meanwhile speculation with land, commodities, and food hasn't only affected people in the third world, it's affected everyone. There are only protected zones for the super rich, but they too will lose everything if money becomes worthless overnight.

But why is this happening? What for?

It's simple – because it serves the satisfaction of a human impulse: greed. A greed that we all share, regardless of whether we are investment bankers or laborers, property-holders or propertyless, rich or poor. Everyone wants more.

Human beings however, have the ability to experience more than just greed, as I described at the beginning of the book; we also have a good sense of fairness, and we have understanding. And if we give it just a little consideration, we will all see that it can't go on this way forever.

There is no other way than to invite vision, to invite the unfamiliar because after one of the next crises, the Great Crisis, the "run-of-the-mill" will stop.

So why not now?

Because everyone who is saving money, who owns a home, has a job, everyone living in the developed countries is afraid – afraid that someone will take something away from them. Afraid of being tricked and cheated. Afraid of dying.

Death will come, but at least it won't be from starvation – that's something that stays in the third world. But this has to be clear: Even if the vision of a fair economic order were instituted right now, it would take a few generations before the world became more just. Until then, some will be drinking champagne while others have to be satisfied with cholera-contaminated water.

Some will speculate while others die.

What's stopping you personally from taking part in this vision – a vision that has no losers, only winners?

Consider this while you read the rest of this book. Consider this while your money is making money in the bank of your choice, or in your pension fund. While your money, through intricate channels, is becoming blood money, money that people are dying over. And give yourself plenty of time for your thoughts, because you know: "Where blood lines the streets is where the most money will be made."[62] Your money: the money that you need for your retirement, the money for later, the money you need to feel relaxed and safe.

Should there be some sympathy for your particular, personal situation?

Then you haven't understood my vision for a fair economic order. No one loses, there are only winners.

What Distribution of Land has to do with the New Money

He who wants to accomplish justice
can give no consideration to the personal interests of the moguls.[63]

Anselm von Feuerbach
(founder of the modern German criminal law doctrine, 1775–1833)

Money is elusive, it can't be grasped. It can be portioned out and then in the blink of an eye it can accumulate somewhere else. Except for cash, it has no material that can be grasped, it has no substance and can multiply itself arbitrarily. It is virulent. Nevertheless, it promises us that it can transform into substance anywhere on the globe, that it can materialize. This promise, and its qualities of never losing value and bearing no storage costs, allow it to rule the world. That works because everyone believes in it, even if the stability of money is an illusion.

Owning land is very different: It can't move; instead it stays put, anchored to the earth. Land cannot multiply itself. It is unambiguously limited, at least until we are able to settle on other planets. For land to be tangible, we don't need to believe in it – we just need to put our feet on the ground. It's there: as hills, lakes, fields, cities, etc. land is the actual substance behind money.

Without land, all money would be worthless.

Land and water nourish us. The pre-products of all goods go back to raw materials that are either trapped, bred, harvested, or dug out of the earth. Most services, too, need a space where they can be performed.

Land and money are inseparably intertwined.

Imagine the monetary reform with money that gradually depreciates, but without a land reform. The only possibility for the old money to keep its value is to be invested in land. And this presents a major problem, because unlike gold and diamond dealers, who would be stupid to trade their goods for gradually depreciating money, land is relatively unprotected. Where land is available, it would come to the bloodiest land seizures in the history of humanity.

In that case, we could spare ourselves the monetary reform. The result would be that a few of the richest people would own all of the land in the world. They are trying to do that now, but if a monetary reform were to take place, this dynamic would develop a speed that would exponentially increase the gap between land owners and the landless. Despite a well-meant and just monetary reform, the gap between rich and poor would widen.

This is where the beginning of the vision for a new economic order takes shape: All changes to the global economy that do not endeavor to establish permanent equal opportunity between rich and poor will fail.

If, however, we keep going as we have been – fighting and avoiding a fair distribution of land, an unconditional worldwide basic income, an equitable relationship between goods and money through gradually depreciating money – then we can forget about all other global projects as well. That includes all ecological projects, measures against global warming, projects for distributing and developing water resources, health, education and food projects – everything really that is at the top of the world's agenda.

Global Problems Require Global Solutions

Civilization means helping each other,
individuals helping individuals, nations helping nations.[64]

Henry Dunant
(founder of the International Red Cross movement, Nobel Peace
Prize recipient, 1828–1910)

We have a global economy, we live in a globalized world, and no one can turn back the wheel of history. Globalization is a result of the division of labor and the only way to get around it would be one hundred percent self-sufficiency.

Division of labor makes sense; people are different and have different abilities, each is a specialist in his or her own area. The fact that many people are unable to experience their inherent potential has nothing to do with their abilities; it is caused by economic conditions. The Indian day laborers described in the introduction of this book might have the potential to be gifted mathematicians or economists. The reason that they can't experience this and share it with the world is only that they were born in the wrong time and the wrong place.

Let's not have any illusions: Specialization was developed in the long course of human history, and it is a characteristic of freedom to be allowed to experience these special abilities without needing to be entirely self-sufficient.

If we look at nature and its resources, we see a situation similar to the diversity of human abilities: In Germany and the Sahara, oranges don't grow. Oil doesn't gush in Switzerland. If we look back at the economy, we see that at the moment the United States is lacking in gas-efficient cars, that Switzerland lacks skilled laborers, and that the third world lacks machines to refine the resources that are found there.

Why should we turn back the wheel of globalization if it allows us to solve existing difficulties?

If you look back at the world agenda described in the last chapter, you'll see that all of the top issues affect the entire world's population and not just a few countries. We have a lot of global problems, and we can only solve them globally. It doesn't make sense to complain about globalization or to be afraid of it – we need to use it for global land reform and for the introduction of money with gradual depreciation.

Both only work globally.

At the beginning, I made reference to the fact that the visions I describe are a lot older than I am and that they go back to the French economist Pierre-Joseph Proudhon, the Belgian-Argentinian businessman Johann Silvio Gesell, and the British economist John Maynard Keynes.

The creative time of the oldest of these economists, Proudhon, began around 1850 and the most recent, Keynes, died in 1946. The reason that many of their ideas for a fair economic order were forgotten or relegated to small intellectual circles is related to the fact that their visions were not global. That wasn't possible because times were different. Proudhon lived before the First World War, Gesell survived it, and Keynes died one year after the Second World War. The view of the economy and its interconnection with politics was different than it is today; and many of these economists' theses only start to make sense in a global environment.

The preservers of the pure doctrine will naturally take exception to these statements. For example, some of Gesell's works are in vogue with opponents of globalization, and the model of regional currencies is also based on his work. With Keynes, on the other hand, many people only think of the current discussion about stimulus programs and about how much influence the state should have on the economy because few people have read and understood his work in detail. And Proudhon is totally "out;" he aligned himself with anarchism in the middle of his life. However, even if these economists' works are very dry and to some extent written in old-fashioned language, they are more relevant than ever today.

In reading them, we shouldn't forget that we live in a global world with global problems that require global solutions. Regional currencies are working hard, but they certainly won't solve a global finance and distribution crisis. The world that I dream of is not regional, it's global, and in it not only money and goods but people too can move freely and unhindered.

But the most important thing is: This world is fair.

Up until now this has only existed in science fiction films like Star Trek where the question of money can be answered with shake of the head: "We work to better ourselves and the rest of humanity,"[65] and everyone works according to their own needs and abilities.

The Realization

I have a dream.[66]

Martin Luther King
(American civil rights activist, 1929–1968)

I promised to describe a vision of a fair economic order and I hope that I was able to do so. Alongside its fundamental ideas, however, a vision must include at least a few practical proposals for its realization; and I would like to present a few of these to you in the following section. These continuing thoughts are, however, still not fully ripened and may seem at many points to be native; so please take them only as proposals.

The first question in the vision of a fair economic order is the sequence of the several major programs that are necessary for its realization. As in everything that has been described, there is a logical order here as well.

The first step is the introduction of a world currency – one without the gradual depreciation of the new money.

The global community has experience with currency reforms and currency confederations. The euro was introduced across the borders of many countries, and without every country having to follow the same economic policies. There was also the collapse of the German Democratic Republic with its worthless currency, the ostmark, and the introduction of the German mark. There are examples of currency devaluations and of parallel currencies. Ultimately, however, there is already a global currency, even if many people resist and disavow it: It is the US dollar, and we can't get around it despite all justifiable objections and the USA's exorbitantly high over-indebtedness: not the Europeans, Russians, Australians, Indians, or South Americans, not the Chinese as the greatest believers in the United States, and not the African countries either. The question whether that is right, and whether it doesn't exonerate a country that has lived far beyond its means is beside the point because we have no other solution. The euro, at least, can be written off: Its well-meant stability criteria[i] make it too inflexible to be a world currency.

Once we have a common currency, we don't necessarily have to print new money right away, but only freeze the exchange rate and stop money printing worldwide. Skeptics may note at this point that the European Currency Unit, the Europe-wide unit of account, existed long before the euro.

The second step would be the land reform and the realization of a worldwide unconditional basic income. Here too we have already had ample experience with transborder leasing and tenancy agreements. We aren't moving into new territory, but within the familiar capitalist system.

The difficulties here are in the distribution of the worldwide basic income because it requires that every citizen in the world somehow be registered. I can hear the data security specialists calling out: That is the gateway to surveillance society! This danger exists, but can data protection really be a reason to hinder the elimination of hunger in the world? Haven't we become a little over-sensitive to this issue in the western developed countries? The issue is still global fairness – it is about the distribution of the unconditional worldwide basic income. Concerns are important, but too many concerns stop every reform.

The last step in the realization would be the introduction of gradual inflation. For deposit money, money that is in accounts or floating around the globe, this is no problem because all payment flows are processed electronically. Money being added to that money through interest or taken out and eliminated is no great technical challenge. Every Y2K project was more complex than that.

---

[i] The euro was introduced as a currency in the third stage of the European Economic and Monetary Union. Countries that want to use it must fulfill the very strict provisions of the so-called Maastricht criteria. These criteria have proven too be too strict in many cases even for stable national economies. There are also some double standards applied to the political and economic importance of a country within the European Union.

For paper money and coins, it is a bit more difficult.[i]

Here too there are tried models, for example the Stamp Scrip from the monetary experiment in the thirties in the Austrian town Wörgl: In 1932 things were looking bleak in Wörgl. High unemployment and dramatic indebtedness were plaguing the 4,200 inhabitants of the Austrian town. In this situation the mayor, Michael Unterguggenberger, proposed to the town council that they try a monetary experiment that the economist Silvio Gesell had described. In an emergency aid program, it was decided that "Wörgler Freigeld" be introduced, so-called Certified Compensation Bills that were backed by bills and shillings. This new money had a distinctive feature: People who collected and held the Freigeld at the bank accrued no interest. Moreover, at the end of every month a usage fee had to be paid – a negative interest, if you like, that penalized anyone who hoarded money. The results of this small-town experiment were visible: The impetus to spend the Freigeld as quickly as possible led to fluid monetary circulation. A large amount of investments had the effect of reducing unemployment by a quarter, while it continued to rise elsewhere. Wörgl could even afford a ski jump. Even as the neighboring community of Kirchbichl wanted to follow the example, the National Bank in Vienna was upset and ended this experiment in eliminating interest before the Austrian Higher Administrative Court.[67]

You can see that there are examples here as well, and that there was even a successful experiment.

Once all of the steps have been taken toward the realization of a fair economic order, it will take ten to fifteen years until all of the speculative money has disappeared from the market – according to the devaluation rate, which is to be duly decided by the World Authority for Currency and Land. After this happens, we can just sit back and wait. Since there will be no more great impetus for speculation, purely speculative money will disappear by itself from speculative funds without creating any new bubbles.

---

[i] The big question is: Do we even need paper money and coins? After the worldwide unconditional basic income is introduced, it will need to reach its recipients, and that will probably take place without cash. Every citizen in the world will therefore have an account, no matter what type. There are also many current examples of using biometric characteristics for definite identification (fingerprints, iris scanners). Why, then, shouldn't the good old wallet at some point become fully electronic – the slide-rule was given up about forty years ago in favor of the calculator and telegraphy about twenty years ago in favor of email and later text messaging.

Much more important is the question of how the land reform and the worldwide unconditional basic income can have a permanent effect. A transformation of the current distribution of the world into a fair and just distribution will certainly take a few generations. Those who initiate the reforms will not live to see the blossoming of its effects. It was a similar case for landscape gardeners in the Middle Ages: Only later generations could enjoy the true beauty of their creations.

In this sense, the third way will remain a vision – something that I can only describe for people to either embrace or reject.

It is a dream.

But sometimes, dreams are fulfilled more quickly than we might believe. On August 28, 1963, less than half a century ago, Martin Luther King spoke in Washington D.C. before 250,000 people in one of his most famous speeches about his dream that racial separation would disappear and that white and black Americans could live in equality with one another.

Five years later, on April 4, 1968 Martin Luther King was shot in Memphis Tennessee. But the wheel of history couldn't be stopped – it kept turning. Since January 20, 2009, the 44th president of the United States has been a man named Barack Hussein Obama. He is the first African-American to take this office, and that is more than Martin Luther King ever dared to dream.

About the Author

Rainer Grunert is one of Germany's new lateral thinker in nonfiction. Born in 1958, he began his professional life as a typesetter and later studied business economics and psychology. After several additional studies, travels abroad, and an internet start-up company, he joined an international consultancy firm. He specialized there in strategic financial restructuring and information technology. In 2000, he became a freelancer and worked for six years as a temporary manager and a consultant for the management of large corporations. Since 2007, Rainer Grunert has worked as an author and a coach with a private practice in Zurich.

More information is available at: www.rainergrunert.com

Publications in German language

2008   Leiden oder Leidenschaft (Textbook on Couple Therapy)

2009   Anleitung zum wunschlosen Glück (Essay)

2009   Vision einer fairen Wirtschaftsordnung (Essay)

2012   Sisyphos Jailbreak (Novel)

References

Arnold, Lutz G.: *Business Cycle Theory.* Oxford 2002.

Atwood, Margaret: *Payback.* Berlin 2008

Brandt Hartmut, Otzen Uwe: "Bodenreform – Voraussetzung aller Entwicklung." in: *Entwicklung und Zusammenarbeit,* nr. 11, November 2002, pp. 304-308.

Brecht, Bertolt: *Die Dreigroschenoper.* Aarau 2004.

Creutz, Helmut: *Die 29 Irrtümer rund ums Geld.* Vienna 2008.

Darwin, Charles: *Die Abstammung des Menschen.* Paderborn 2005.

Färber, Heinrich: *Die Irrlehre Silvio Gesells.* Graz 1996.

Fisher, Irving: *The Money Illusion.* Whitefish 2006.

Gerdesmeier, Dieter: *Geldtheorie und Geldpolitik.* Frankfurt 2004.

Gesell, Silvio: *Das Monopol der schweizerischen Nationalbank und die Grenzen der Geldausgabe im Falle einer Sperrung der freien Goldausprägung.* Bern 1901.

Gesell, Silvio: *Die Anpassung des Geldes und seiner Verwaltung an die Bedürfnisse des modernen Verkehrs.* Buenos Aires 1897.

Gesell, Silvio: *Gesammelte Werke.* Kiel 1988.

Gischer Horst; Herz, Bernard; Menkhoff, Lukas: *Geld, Kredit, Banken.* Berlin 2005.

Goethe, Johann Wolfgang von: *Faust: Der Tragödie erster und zweiter Teil.* München 2007.

Goethe, Johann Wolfgang von: *Maximen und Reflektionen.* Cologne

Hemmer, Hans-Rimbert; Frenkel, Michael: *Grundlagen der Wachstumstheorie.* München 1999.

Kasper, Hans: *Abel, gib acht. Halbzeit der Emanzipationen.* Düsseldorf 1962.

Kennedy, Margrit: *Geld ohne Zinsen und Inflation.* München 1994.

Keynes, John Maynard: *A Tract on Monetary Reform.* New York 2000.

Keynes, John Maynard: *Allgemeine Theorie der Beschäftigung, des Zinses und des Geldes.* Berlin 1994.

King, Martin Luther: *Warum wir nicht warten können.* Berlin 1964.

Krishnamurti, Jiddu: *Freiheit und wahres Glück.* Munich 2007.

Kuhn, Berthold: *Entwicklungspolitik zwischen Markt und Staat.* Frankfurt 2005.

Laotse: *Tao Te King* (new German translation by Peter Kobbe). Munich, 2003.

Martin, Hans-Peter; Schumann, Harald: *Die Globalisierungsfalle.* Reinbek 1996.

Marx, Karl: *Das Kapital.* Leipzig 2007.

Marx, Karl: *Lohnarbeit und Kapital – Lohn, Preis und Profit.* Berlin 1998.

Otte, Max: *Der Crash kommt.* Berlin 2006.

PNAS: "Neidische Hunde." in: *Spektrum der Wissenschaft* 2/2009
(http://www.spektrum.de/artikel/979391).

Proudhon, Pierre-Joseph: *System der ökonomischen Widersprüche oder: Philosophie des Elends.* Berlin 2003.

Proudhon, Pierre-Joseph: *Was ist das Eigentum?* Vienna 1992.

Rawls, John: *Eine Theorie der Gerechtigkeit.* Frankfurt 2003.

Schopenhauer, Arthur: *Die Welt als Wille und Vorstellung.* Munich 1998.

Schwarz, Fritz: *Das Experiment von Wörgl.* Darmstadt 2008.

Senf, Bernd: *Die blinden Flecken der Ökonomie.* Munich 2001.

Smith, Adam: *Der Reichtum der Nationen.* Paderborn 2005.

Stiglitz, Joseph E.: *Die Chancen der Globalisierung.* Berlin 2006.

Wilson D. S. und Wilson E. O.: "Evolution – Gruppe oder Individuum?" in: *Spektrum der Wissenschaft* 1/2009.

Footers

[1] Quoted in: Das, Lama Surya: *Awakening the Buddha Within. Tibetan Wisdom for the Western World.* New York 1998, p. 146.

[2] Quoted in: Radermacher, Franz Joseph: *Global Marshall Plan: A Planetary Contract* Global Marshall Plan Intiative (Ed.) 2004, p. 146.
http://files.globalmarshallplan.org/gmp_text/global_marshall_plan_e_I_eng.pdf,.
pdf

[3] Rainer Grunert: *Leiden oder Leidenschaft.* Innenwelt Verlag, Cologne 2008, and *Anleitung zum wunschlosen Glück.* Windpferd Verlag, Oberstdorf 2009.

[4] (Translation) Ger. orig: "Es mag einfacher sein, ein Land zu regieren, als eine Stromrechnung zu lesen." Elke Dünnhoff: "Strom sparen im Alltag – ganz einfach! Aber warum macht das keiner?" In: Institute for Energy and Environment Research Heidelberg (Ed.): *Klimawandel und Alltagshandeln.* Meeting of Heinrich-Böll-Stiftung Hessen e.V. on 10/28/2006 in Marburg; see: http://www.hbs-hes-sen.de/fileadmin/HBS/Themen/Duennhoff_ifeu_Stromsparen_Vortrag_fin.pdf (last page).

[5] Keynes, John Maynard: *A Tract on Monetary Reform.* New York 2000.

[6] (Translation) Ger. orig: "Die Menschen verdrießt's, dass das Wahre so einfach ist, sie sollten bedenken, dass sie noch Mühe genug haben, es praktisch zu ihrem Nutzen anzuwenden." Goethe, Johann Wolfgang. *Maximen und Reflektionen.* Munich 2006, p. 159.

[7] Ger.:Rawls, John: *Eine Theorie der Gerechtigkeit.* Frankfurt 2003.

[8] Ger.: Smith, Adam: *Der Reichtum der Nationen.* Paderborn 2005.

[9] https://www.cia.gov/library/publications/the-world-factbook/index.html.

[10] http://www.worldbank.org/.

[11] www.imf.org.

[12] www.un.org.

[13] http://www.highbeam.com/doc/1P1-98936838.html.

[14] (Translation) Ger. orig: "Denn alles Streben entspringt aus Mangel, aus Unzufriedenheit mit seinem Zustand – ist also Leiden, solange es nicht befriedigt ist. Keine Befriedigung aber ist dauernd, vielmehr ist sie nur der Anfangspunkt eines neuen Strebens." Schopenhauer, Arthur: *Die Welt als Wille und Vorstellung.* Munich 1998, p. 398. Engl: http://www.sebastianhayes.co.uk/?p=48.

[15] (Translation) Ger. orig: "Die Menschen träumen vom leistungslosen Einkommen, sie wollen reich sein, aber das gratis. " Peter Sloterdijk, cited in *Focus* 2/2009, "Sprüche der Woche".

[16] http://www.jkrishnamurti.org/krishnamurti-teachings/view-text.php?tid=14&chid=153&w=

[17] (Translation) Ger. orig: "Innerhalb der eigenen Horde sind anständige Menschen gegenüber unredlichen nicht erkennbar im Vorteil. Allerdings werden Horden aus anständigen Menschen andere Gruppen klar übertrumpfen. Das ist natürliche Selektion." Darwin, Charles: *Die Abstammung des Menschen*. Taken from: Wilson D.S. und Wilson E.O.: "Evolution – Gruppe oder Individuum?" in *Spektrum der Wissenschaft* 1/2009.

[18] PNAS: "Neidische Hunde" in *Spektrum der Wissenschaft* 2/2009.

[19] Wilson D.S. and Wilson E.O.: "Evolution – Gruppe oder Individuum?" in *Spektrum der Wissenschaft* 1/2009.

[20] (Translation) Ger. orig: "Die Humanität erreichte mehr, wenn sie, statt die Gleichheit zu loben, zum Respekt vor dem Wunder der Vielfalt riete." Kasper, Hans: *Abel, gib acht. Halbzeit der Emanzipationen*. Düsseldorf 1962.

[21] Ger.: http://de.wikipedia.org/wiki/Fairness.

[22] Ger.: http://europa.eu/agencies/community_agencies/frontex/index_de.htm .

[23]

http://www.proasyl.de/fileadmin/proasyl/fm_redakteure/Flyer_PDF/FRONTEX.pdf.

http://torun.indymedia.org/4829.

http://frontex.antira.info/.

http://thecaravan.org/node/1360.

http://www.netzwerk-regenbogen.de/asylfl071225.html.

[24] http://en.wikipedia.org/wiki/Small_world_experiment

[25] (Translation) Ger.: "Erkennst du klar, dass sich alle Dinge verändern, dann wirst du an nichts festhalten wollen. " Laotse: *Tao Te King* (New translation by Peter Kobbe). Munich, 2003, p. 80 (Nr. 74).

[26] (Translation) Ger. orig: "Alle Liberalen dieser Welt sind der Meinung, dass Grenzen offen sein sollten: für Güter, für Geld und für Dienstleistungen. Schwieriger wird es bei Menschen, da muss man sich überlegen, ob man nicht eine Art Eintrittspreis verlangt, so wie man eben in einem Klub auch Eintrittspreise verlangt." Schwarz, Dr. Gerhard: in an interview in the film "Let's make Money" by Erwin Wagenhofer.

[27] (Translation) Ger. orig: "Die FAO (Food and Agriculture Organization of the United Nations) richtete Ende der siebziger Jahre die ständige Weltkonferenz für Agrarreform und ländliche Entwicklung ein, die leider ihrer Aufgabe nicht gerecht werden konnte. Bis heute stehen Bodenreformen auf der politischen Aufgabenliste vieler Entwicklungsländer. Bodenreformen lassen sich definieren als Änderungen der Institutionen der Bodennutzung und des Bodenbesitzes sowie Neuaufteilung landwirtschaftlicher Betriebsflächen, durchgeführt von den Herrschenden, um

wirtschaftliche und politische Widersprüchlichkeiten und Konflikte zu überwinden, ohne die dominanten sozialen Strukturen und Beziehungsgeflechte zu verändern." Brandt Hartmut, Otzen Uwe: "Bodenreform – Voraussetzung aller Entwicklung" in *Entwicklung und Zusammenarbeit* (Nr. 11, November 2002, p. 304–308). Autor's note: This text comes from 2002. There has been no noteworthy progress since then, and so the text is as up-to-date as when it first appeared.

[28] Plato: *De legibus.* Chapter XI. Engl: Yunis, Harvey. *Taming Democracy: Models of Political Rhetoric in Classical Athens.* New York 1996, p. 229. Google Book Search.

[29] Jean-Jacques Rousseau: *Emile* 4. Engl: William, David Lay: *Rousseau's Platonic Enlightenment.* University Park 2007, p. 74. Google Book Search.

[30] (Translation) Ger. orig: "Etwas von seinem Eigentume fahren lassen, sein Recht aufgeben – macht Freude, wenn es großen Reichtum anzeigt. Dahin gehört die Großmut." Nietzsche, Friedrich: *Morgenröte.* Fourth book. "Sich entäußern."

[31] http://en.wikipedia.org/wiki/Leaseback.

[32] http://en.wikipedia.org/wiki/Cross-border_leasing.

[33] http://en.wikiquote.org/wiki/Martin_Luther_King,_Jr.

[34] See http://legal-dictionary.thefreedictionary.com/One+Person,+One+Vote: "The principle that all citizens, regardless of where they reside in a state, are entitled to equal legislative representation. This principle was enunciated by the Supreme Court in Reynolds v. Sims, 377 U.S. 533, 84 S. Ct. 1362, 12 L. Ed. 2d 506 (1964). The Court ruled that a state's Apportionment plan for seats in both houses of a bicameral state legislature must allocate seats on a population basis so that the voting power of each voter be as equal as possible to that of any other voter."

[35] http://en.wikipedia.org/wiki/Purchasing_power_parity.

[36] (Translation) Ger. orig: "Henry Ford hat einmal gesagt, er müsse seinen Arbeitern einen vernünftigen Lohn bezahlen, damit sie in der Lage seien, seine Autos zu kaufen. Wenn sich die Weltwirtschaft nicht erholt, werden die Exportländer auch ihre Waren nicht mehr verkaufen können." Strauss-Kahn, Dominique: "Einige Staaten stehen bereits Schlange." In *Die Zeit* 06/09.

[37] (Translation) Ger.: Pascal, Blaise: *Gedanken* (257). Engl: Pascal, Blaise. *Thoughts on Religion and Philosopy.* Trans. Isaac Taylor. Glasgow 1838, p. 393. Google Book Search.

[38] (Translation) Ger. orig: "Zuerst kommt das Fressen, und dann kommt die Moral." Brecht, Bertolt: *Die Dreigroschenoper.* Aarau 2004.

[39] (Translation) Ger. orig: "Es gibt Besserwisser, die niemals begreifen, dass man Recht haben und doch ein Idiot sein kann." http://zitate.de/ergebnisse.php?autor=&kategorie=Besserwisser, Zitat-Nr. 1348.

[40] http://de.wikipedia.org/wiki/Bevölkerungswachstum and http://de.wikipedia.org/wiki/Weltbevölkerung.

[41] (Translation) Ger.: Keynes, John Maynard: Allgemeine Theorie der Beschäfti-

gung, des Zinses und des Geldes. Berlin 1994. Engl.: Keynes, John Maynard. *The General Theory of Employment, Interest and Money*. Delhi 2006. Google Books Search.

[42] (Translation) Ger. orig.: "Die schlimmste Wirkung des Kapitalismus ist, dass man glaubt, alles, was man bezahlen kann, gehöre einem." http://www.zitate.de/detail-autor-5129.htm.

[43] http://de.wikipedia.org/wiki/Alan_Greenspan.

[44] Greenspan, Alan: 1987 Address to the US Congress, *The San Francisco Chronicle*, 9 June 1995, cited in German at: http://de.wikiquote.org/wiki/Alan_Greenspan. Engl. orig: http://www.wordspy.com/WAW/Greenspan-Alan.asp.

[45] (Translation) Ger. orig: "Herr, die Not ist groß! Die ich rief, die Geister, werd ich nun nicht mehr los." Goethe, Johann Wolfgang von: *Faust: Der Tragödie erster und zweiter Teil*. München 2007. Engl.: http://en.wikiquote.org/wiki/Johann_Wolfgang_von_Goethe.

[46] http://de.wikipedia.org/wiki/Dotcom-Blase.

[47] http://de.wikipedia.org/wiki/OPEC.

[48] http://de.biz.yahoo.com/30052008/390/kommende-weltwaehrung-amero-zwischenstufe.html – der verdeckte Dollar-Öl-Standard.

[49] http://www.freitag.de/2006/08/06080702.php.

[50] (Translation) Ger.: "So ist der Wucher hassenswert, weil er aus dem Geld selbst den Erwerb zieht und nicht aus dem, wofür das Geld da ist. Denn das Geld ist um des Tausches willen erfunden worden, durch den Zins vermehrt es sich dagegen durch sich selbst." Aristotle: *Politik*.. 1. Buch, 1259 a. Engl.: http://en.wikipedia.org/wiki/Politics_(Aristotle).

[51] Ger.: http://de.wikipedia.org/wiki/Zins

[52] Ger.: http://de.wikiquote.org/wiki/Gehen. Engl: Rohsenow, John S. *ABC Dictionary of Chinese Proverbs* Hawaii 2003. Google Books Search.

[53] Ger.: http://de.wikipedia.org/wiki/Zins

[54] (Translation) Ger. orig.: Goethe, Johann Wolfgang von: *Faust: Der Tragödie erster und zweiter Teil*. München 2007. Engl.: http://en.wikiquote.org/wiki/Johann_Wolfgang_von_Goethe.

[55] Keynes, John Maynard: *A Tract on Monetary Reform*. New York 2000.

[56] Dr. Mark Mobius, investor, Emerging Markets Fund Manager, Managing Director of Templeton Asset Management Ltd., Singapur, in an interview in the film "Let's Make Money" by Erwin Wagenhofer.

[57] (Translation) Ger. orig: "Hungersnöte brechen nicht aus, sie werden gemacht." Brecht, Bertolt: Die heilige Johanna der Schlachthöfe. Frankfurt 1960.

[58] (Translation) Ger. orig: "Inflation ist wie Nikotin oder Alkohol. In kleinem Maße ist es stimulierend, man darf nur kein Kettenraucher werden oder Alkoholiker." http://www.gutzitiert.de/zitat_thema_inflation.html.

[59] Ger.: http://natune.net/zitate/zitat/7328.

[60] Ger.: http://www.zitate.de/ergebnisse.php?kategorie=Vision#1. Engl.: Aristotle, trans. Samuel Henry Butcher. *Poetics*. Whitefish, MT, USA 2009. Google Books search.

[61] (Translation) Ger. orig.: "Alles, von dem sich der Mensch eine Vorstellung machen kann, ist machbar."
http://www.zitate.de/db/ergebnisse.php?kategorie=Vision.

[62] Dr. Mark Mobius, investor, Emerging Markets Fund Manager, Managing Director of Templeton Asset Management Ltd., Singapur, in an interview in the film "Let's Make Money" by Erwin Wagenhofer.

[63] (Translation) Ger. orig: "Wer Gerechtigkeit durchsetzen will, darf keine Rücksicht nehmen auf die persönlichen Interessen der Großen." http://www.nur-zitate.com/autor/Anselm_Paul_Johann_Ritter_von_Feuerbach.html.

[64] (Translation) Ger. orig: "Zivilisation bedeutet, sich gegenseitig zu helfen von Mensch zu Mensch, von Nation zu Nation." http://www.nur-zitate.com/autor/Anselm_Paul_Johann_Ritter_von_Feuerbach.html.

[65] http://en.wikiquote.org/wiki/Work.

[66] http://en.wikipedia.org/wiki/I_Have_a_Dream.

[67] For info. in German on this topic, see:
http://www.zeit.de/2003/06/Zinsgeschichte; Schwarz, Fritz: *Das Experiment von Wörgl*. Darmstadt 2008; http://de.wikipedia.org/wiki/Wörgl and http://neuesgeld.com/page.php?id=22. Eng. text sourced from:
http://en.wikipedia.org/wiki/Wörgl